THE NEW ANALYST'S GUIDE
TO THE GALAXY

THE NEW ANALYST'S GUIDE TO THE GALAXY

Questions about Contemporary Psychoanalysis

Antonino Ferro and Luca Nicoli

Translated by Adriano Bompani

KARNAC

First published in 2017 by
Karnac Books Ltd
118 Finchley Road
London NW3 5HT

British Library Cataloguing in Publication Data

A C.I.P. for this book is available from the British Library

ISBN-13: 978-1-78220-542-5

Typeset by V Publishing Solutions Pvt Ltd., Chennai, India

Printed in Great Britain

www.karnacbooks.com

"I would like to understand."

"What?"

"Everything, all this."

I gestured toward my surroundings.

"You'll understand when you've forgotten what you understood before."

— *Italo Calvino*, The Origin of the Birds

CONTENTS

ABOUT THE AUTHORS

Antonino Ferro is a training and supervising analyst in the Italian Psychoanalytical Society (SPI), of which he is the president, the American Psychoanalytic Association (APsaA), and the International Psychoanalytical Association (IPA). He has been a visiting professor of psychoanalysis in various institutions in Europe, North America, South America, and Australia. He received the Sigourney Award in 2007.

Luca Nicoli, psychologist and psychoanalyst, is member of the Italian Psychoanalytical Society and of the International Psychoanalytical Association. He is a member of the editorial board of the *Rivista di Psicoanalisi* (Italian Psychoanalytic Journal). His three books are published in Italian: *Amare senza perdersi* (Loving without Losing Ourselves, 2009), *L'Arte di arrabbiarsi* (The Art of Getting Angry, 2012), and *Il Sogno* (The Dream, 2014).

An anthology of uncomfortable thoughts

"Do you still use the couch?"

"What if we worked in tandem? You explain to your patients where their problems come from, and then I help them through counselling."

"Doctor, I need to talk about my present. You don't just deal with the past, right?"

Every day, at work or when visiting friends, I notice how today psychoanalysis is seen as an intellectual, somewhat old-fashioned exercise, a quirk for nostalgics who want to be pampered (or dissected) for years on end, while their life goes on unaffected.

The intense prejudice currently weighing upon the discipline that I'm most passionate about, to which I sacrificed years of study, effort, and money, is surely the result of today's impatience with traditional institutions, neglected in favour of more fashionable approaches. However, psychoanalysts share some of the guilt for this, too.

Like many revolutions that become regimes, our discipline, born as a cultural scandal—giving voice to the sexual urges of utterly virtuous bourgeois gentlewomen, above all—over time struggled to maintain its innovative energy. Many analysts have chosen to risk immobilising psychoanalysis in the formal rigour that is now familiar to most, rather than to let it run wild, fearing it would lose its soul. And so we got the sarcastic cartoons that, wrongly or rightly, depict an analyst who sits perfectly silent, or even falls asleep, while his poor patient pours rivers of tears upon his sufferings.

Meanwhile, in reality, the international psychoanalytic movement has come a long way. Working with adolescents and infants enabled the development of new, more direct and colloquial ways to approach patients. Likewise, patients suffering from the most serious illnesses forced analysts to revise and expand their toolbox.

I am deeply saddened by the fact that little has been done to divulge this slow cultural revolution to the outside. Maybe because it is hard for successors to overshadow such a burdensome father as Freud, maybe because analysts fear oversimplifying their concepts by using mass media or by writing for the general public; either way many today see psychoanalysis as a dusty oddity.

So, what about all the curious people who hope to meet someone who could lead them on a voyage within themselves, without being too scared?

And what about the new analysts of today and tomorrow, who want to listen to the dreams and to accept the other without being forced to resort to behavioural techniques? Many of them are temporary workers in healthcare or academia, or even bartenders and waiters, working the night shift to pay for their studies and analysis, donning the mantle of the therapist for a few hours during the day; freelancers with patients who come and go (and when they go, they leave so many doubts about your mistakes …), all of them supported by a passion that's hard to understand from the outside.

This guide is dedicated to these dreamers.

A book that is a bit of a guide, a bit of a tongue-in-cheek handbook, a bit of a walk in the study of a great analyst as we watch, unseen, what happens inside.

I became the first watcher when I approved Antonino Ferro's idea to weave a dialogue between a new analyst and a world-famous master, made-to-measure for those who are curious about contemporary psychoanalysis.

Honestly, I had no idea what was in store for me.

I spent a month hunting for questions, notebook in hand. During the sessions, on the street, with my colleagues. Sometimes the questions were the same as ever, repeated to myself so many times they became internalised, almost like mantras. How do you avoid losing patients? How difficult is the transition from the convexity of interpretation to the concavity of attuning? And then the things all new analysts wonder about: what neutrality and how much neutrality, when to use the couch, the number of sessions, money.

The remaining questions were raised in Antonino Ferro's office, as we associated and tied together the threads of the conversation that was taking shape: we ranged between theory and technique, between projective identification, transformations, the value of insight in the healing process, and the choice of characters in the analytic field.

The analytic field, Antonino Ferro's creature, is an extraordinary innovation in psychoanalytic theory. Following in the footsteps of Wilfred Bion, Ferro shifts the analytic work's focus from the revelation of unconscious contents, a process of Freudian origin, to the metaphorical narrative of the relationship between the analyst and the patient. The two subjects of analysis are no longer seen as identities in relation, but rather as two worlds that blend in a relational field, giving life to many scenarios that differ each time. Ferro's psychoanalysis aims to make explicit, through the creation of stories, the hidden aspects of the existing relationship. The patient's inhibited parts, the violent traits hidden inside him, are encouraged to come to light and to meet with the characters that the intuitive and narrative skills of the analyst can create.

As I listened to Ferro's words I felt a strange, unsettling feeling. Something between what I felt as I read Bion's

The Tavistock Seminars and what I felt as I watched Neo, the protagonist of the movie *The Matrix*, wake up in an alien reality, his body pierced by cables.

Shedding the past to head for the future, leaving the already known for what we do not know, without any map or *handbook*.

Yes, I realised there and then that this book would be no handbook. Handbooks provide safety, whereas in the recordings that I was keeping, waiting to pen them down, there were indeed confidence and determination, but also measureless doubts that offered me little solace. They gave me vertigo instead.

Vertigo is not the fear of falling down, but the desire to fly, says a song by Italian singer Jovanotti.

Flying is scary.

Freedom is scary.

The desire for the renewal of psychoanalysis and of its institutions is scary, when it meets a speaker who supports it more than prudence would suggest. There's the risk of going far beyond where one wanted to go. I think of my innate aversion to the monumental Freud who "already said it all", I think of his early psycho-neurological models from the *Project for a Scientific Psychology* that I already consider (unfairly, according to several colleagues) little more than a historical document. I think—I'll say this in a whisper—of *The Interpretation of Dreams* that I never actually read cover to cover, be it for my intellectual laziness, be it for a hint of youthful iconoclastic narcissism, or be it for my feeling that that was the past, albeit a glorious and crucial past. Whereas the present is Glen Gabbard, Thomas Ogden, Boringhieri's now hard-to-find book on dream edited by Stefano Bolognini.

Ferro, with all of his honesty and a bit of recklessness that only those who already have a solid professional background can afford, is suggesting we store all of Freud's work in the institutional vaults.

All of it?

Even *Remembering, Repeating and Working Through*, or *Mourning and Melancholia*, some of the few (yeah …) essays that really impressed me?

At least from the point of view of today's clinical practice and technique, Ferro questions Freud's usefulness, and the father of psychoanalysis might end up definitively becoming a grandfather.[1]

In a blink I found myself defending Freud, or silence in analysis—despite being a lot more chatty than my colleagues in session—defending the rites at the start and end of session that support my perception of being an analyst and not some circus performer.

Maybe it is unavoidable that newcomers, being more scared by the unknown that awaits them and less confident about their toolkit, end up entrenching themselves behind the technique and the already-known of earlier generations.

On the other hand, I felt almost exhilarated by the joy of finding someone who shared with me the vital need for psychoanalysis to look to the future. If the world so stubbornly declares Freud dead every five years or so, as if he was a Paul McCartney, it is probably because we did not properly bury him, we did not try to outlive him while of course honouring him, as we do with our loved ones. Maybe psychoanalysis can still be considered a modern tool of cure, and not a charmingly old-fashioned discipline with shades of religious dogmatism as certain influential international newspapers sometimes depict it, if it manages to overcome its old vices, such as its share of conceptual self-referentiality, its theoretical *ipse dixit*, its founding fathers' and mothers' transference, and a certain cultural snobbery that made it unpopular to many.

For us analysts, above all for the young ones, this is not merely a narcissistic-identitary issue. It is a matter of pursuing a professional and financial investment that is supposed to lead us safely to our retirement age. It is our future we are talking about.

Ferro suggests an extremely seductive method of work, aimed at the future of psychoanalysis.

At times his psychoanalysis looks terribly like "the Dark Side of the Force": tempting, seemingly easy, powerful. It makes one want to immediately become one of his most faithful disciples, to let oneself be tempted; but meanwhile one recoils away from it, because wisdom teaches us that shortcuts do not work in psychoanalysis and idealisations have wings pasted with wax.

The outcome of this brutal conflict was, at least in my case, to open up a third, somewhat uncomfortable dialectic way. I wonder and I'll keep wondering how much certain assumptions correspond to my way of seeing the human being and the analytic couple, to what extent I can give up on transferential, or explicative, interpretations, in favour of a narrative game that fascinates me but at the same time puzzles me.

I think that the readers of this book will, like me, find convincing passages that will make them decidedly nod while reading, whereas elsewhere they will turn up their nose because things look too easy, too radical, or too partisan.

Of course Ferro is partisan.

After growing up in a post-Kleinian cultural context, marked by sharp and punctual, sometimes even aggressive, transferential interpretations, Ferro apparently experienced Bion and his products as a liberating transition: from work *on* the patient to work *with* the patient, our best colleague. He has based his field model on maximum symmetry and collaboration, to an extent that some readers may find excessive, risky, dubious. Likewise his criticism of Freudian theory, for example, may seem excessive.

However, just as Freud can be read and "forgotten", I hope and I think that Ferro wouldn't mind sharing the same fate, becoming a step to bring us a little higher up or, even better, a launch pad for our own personal spacecraft heading towards the unknown of the human mind.

So, let's climb aboard the *"Enterprise"*[2] and let's talk about the guide that we are about to read.

In the popular *The Hitchhiker's Guide to the Galaxy*, whose title we riffed on, the protagonist Arthur Dent wakes up on a Thursday morning just as a huge fleet of spaceships, floating in the sky, announces to Earth's inhabitants that within two minutes the planet is going to be razed to make way for a new hyperspace highway.

It's not the death of psychoanalysis, but close enough.

Only then, as they share a last round of beers before the destruction of the world, Arthur finds out that his drinking buddy, Ford Prefect, is an interplanetary traveller, a hitchhiker, and he can give him "a lift" to new worlds. He needs but bring with him a towel[3] and a copy of the *Guide to the Galaxy*.

While the *Encyclopaedia Galactica* contains every universal notion—much like Etchegoyen's treatise or Laplanche and Pontalis's dictionary—the *Guide* offers ideas, stimuli: how to use a Babel Fish by inserting it into your ear to translate every language in the universe, or which are the best planets to enjoy a glass of Pan Galactic Gargle Blaster, or even how to keep yourself warm while crossing the icy satellites of Jaglan Beta. Likewise our Guide, in its own small way, offers tips on exploring some of the worlds on which we can land in our line of work: erotic transference, negative transference, projective identification, quarrels about the payment of skipped sessions. And lastly …

> … though it has many omissions and contains much that is apocryphal, or at least wildly inaccurate, it [the Guide] scores over the older, more pedestrian work in two important respects.
>
> First, it is slightly cheaper; and second, it has the words "DON'T PANIC" inscribed in large friendly letters on its cover.
>
> (Adams, 1979, p. 2)

Notes

1. I am referencing a speech delivered by Stefano Bolognini, sitting president of the International Psychoanalytical Association, who reaffirmed the need to make Freud "a grandfather" during the Boston 2015 IPA Congress.
2. *USS Enterprise* is the name of the spacecraft from the *Star Trek* TV series. Its crew's mission is "... to explore strange new worlds, to seek out new life and new civilizations, to boldly go where no one has gone before."
3. "*The Hitchhiker's Guide to the Galaxy* has a few things to say on the subject of towels. A towel, it says, is about the most massively useful thing an interstellar hitchhiker can have. Partly it has great practical value. You can wrap it around you for warmth as you bound across the cold moons of Jaglan Beta; you can lie on it on the brilliant marble-sanded beaches of Santraginus V, inhaling the heady sea vapors; you can sleep under it beneath the stars which shine so redly on the desert world of Kakrafoon; use it to sail a miniraft down the slow heavy River Moth; wet it for use in hand-to-hand-combat; wrap it round your head to ward off noxious fumes or avoid the gaze of the Ravenous Bugblatter Beast of Traal (such a mind-bogglingly stupid animal, it assumes that if you can't see it, it can't see you); you can wave your towel in emergencies as a distress signal, and of course dry yourself off with it if it still seems to be clean enough" (Adams, 1979, p. 16).

CHAPTER ONE

Identity

This book is meant to be a self-defence handbook for new, usually young, analysts. What do new analysts have to defend themselves from?

To begin with, I believe that young analysts should defend their opportunity to be young. A few days ago I was reading about an Italian colleague who, in reference to an analyst of sixty-two years, maintained that he had better respect the views of older analysts rather than engage in polemics with them. So an analyst of sixty-two years is still considered a young analyst.

I would hope that young analysts will be, in a matter of not too much time, thirty or thirty-five. That is, that the professional age of the members of psychoanalytic associations can be aligned with their actual age, whereas now there is a twenty, thirty years "bonus" of sorts, so that a young associate is sixty-two years old, a young ordinary is sixty-five, and so on.

And this is a relevant first point. But I'd wager there's more …

Second, I believe that they have to defend themselves from that excess of orthodoxy that prevents developing new ideas,

1

and that is still related to the issue of age. Consider that an analyst who teaches and is more or less around the age of sixty to sixty-five, hard as he tries to keep up to date, has a training that dates back to thirty years before; so, if he teaches in 2016, he teaches 1980s psychoanalysis: there's always a thirty years delay.

In addition to this, I would say that analysts have to defend themselves above all from the psychoanalytic "*Kyrie eleison, Christe eleison*", that is to say from those now completely meaningless formulas that still have to be celebrated as a sign of belonging, and that continually have to be re-proposed to be accepted and recognised as part of the group. This ranges from quoting Freud at the beginning of any work, at least in almost every European country—not so in the USA—to all those things that we take completely for granted. They become acts of faith, keeping us very far from what Bion says in *The Tavistock Seminars* (2005a)—perhaps in quoting him I'm also doing a bit of orthodoxy, an illness from which I will have to sufficiently heal—such as for instance that the concepts of transference and countertransference were so important and have generated so many new thoughts and structures that by now we could easily do without them.

So I believe that all of us, not just new analysts, have to defend ourselves from what we already know: all that is known should not really interest us anymore. If we are convinced that there is an unconscious, or something we call so for now—I hope that in the future it can be replaced by some other concept—and if we intend to concern ourselves with it, then it means that it is the unknown that concerns us. All I know about a patient, once I know it, does not concern me anymore. My gaze, my attention, my ear should be directed towards all that I do not know yet. The same is true regarding psychoanalytic theory: rather than enshrining it or making it an object of uncritical investment, we should begin to set it aside. It's like steps already travelled: obviously we are on the seventh floor thanks to the steps that go from the first to the second, from the second to the third, from the third to the fourth and so on; we feel grateful to the steps that have brought us this far, but we are most concerned with the steps that we have yet to climb in those parts of the building that we still do not know, or that have even yet to be built.

Think of how much orthodoxy obstructs our sight: "Negative transference must always be interpreted!" "Negative transference must be interpreted in this way!" They are too strong assumptions of truth about what we are supposed to do. We should find out each day what would be most useful to do with that patient at that time, depending on how he is and how we are.

Another thing that we should defend ourselves from is the "light pollution" of what we know, that prevents us from seeing still unknown areas, sort of like what happens in the cities, full of night lights. Just think about when we go by plane to New York, at night, and we see huge patches of light, and we know that it is what prevents its citizens from seeing the sky, seeing the stars, seeing the dark. If we go into an area without excessive light instead, we can see a little more of the night. We have too many concepts to which we attach too much importance. I like to mention that it was, aptly enough, two young candidates in psychoanalytic training who pointed out to me something that I had thought for a long time, but had not formulated so clearly. It seems that Arthur Schnitzler, writing on psychoanalysis, stated that the importance attached to the Oedipus complex by psychoanalysis made it impossible to see an overwhelming number of other "complexes", which it would have been possible to notice were it not for this "light pollution" of Oedipus, that makes Oedipus appear everywhere, preventing other constellations from being seen and recognised and made sense of. In other words, just as the "pollution" of what we know about a patient is catastrophic in clinical work, it is equally catastrophic in conceptualisation, while theories and models should be known and then quickly forgotten.

> This brings to my mind another question. If I have to look at the sky to see the stars, I have to know that the sky is above, that I need glasses, if for example I am short-sighted or astigmatic, otherwise I cannot see anything. Then I need some necessary condition, such as darkness, that I can not do without. What are the conditions psychoanalysis needs to remain psychoanalysis— assuming we are concerned with psychoanalysis remaining psychoanalysis? What are the things that we should not forget?

First of all, that the sky is necessarily above remains to be seen, because the sky is also down. I remember how I was blown away, the first time I went to the southern hemisphere, and I saw there was a completely different sky: I was looking for the North Star but I saw the Southern Cross instead. Then, if we imagine drilling a hole through the Earth—thankfully we can imagine anything in psychoanalysis—and through the hole being able to see the other side, the sky would be down. Apart from this oddity, what I mean is that it all depends on the perspective we adopt.

For now I cannot predict how psychoanalysis will look like in a given amount of time; today and in the near future I think that in order to have an analysis we need two individuals and a setting. I think that the minimum necessary is this: that there is an analyst, a patient, and a setting. I am convinced that an analyst can be defined as such when in the company of someone who accepts the position of the patient, in a setting that it makes sense to maintain. Outside this arrangement there is no analyst: I am not an "analyst" from 8 am to 7:59 am the next day, round the clock. I believe that the identity of analyst is something that is acquired only in the presence of the patient and within a setting. In anything we do outside that, we are people who have studied, people with a certain outlook on life. We can possibly use analytical tools, thinking it helps us better understand a movie, a book, but it seems to me that somebody who has anthropological or sociological tools is going to understand them better. My very personal point of view is that we are often ridiculous when we attempt applied psychoanalysis. I think the thing that we are not ridiculous at is being psychoanalysts: just us, our patient, and our setting. Then we become something truly important: people who are able to cope with mental suffering, to take care of it, to heal it, and metabolise it. Our field is the mental suffering of a tormented mind, to which we can certainly bring relief, help, and that we can speed towards a healing process. Obviously, the healing is always relative and always with a lower case "h", but this is our field, this is our specialty.

> So, we both belong to that group of psychoanalysts, and I think they are a majority, who believe that psychoanalysis is above all healing. As dispensers of healing, for over a century psychoanalysts have questioned what are the therapeutic factors. Today there are many other tools of psychological healing: cognitive-behavioral, constructivist, and systemic therapies. I think that it is really important, both for a new analyst in development and for an analyst who has been questioning for all his life, to understand what is the specific function of psychoanalysis as a tool of healing. What is the specific help that an analyst can give to those who turn to him?

I would say: unconscious, unconscious, unconscious.

There is no psychoanalysis if we do not account for the unconscious dimension. Regardless of whether we understand it in its more traditional, Freudian versions, as an already structured, existing unconscious to decipher—which are the earliest, most naïve ways of thinking of the unconscious—or we think of the unconscious as a structure in perennial formation and transformation, in development, so that together with the patient we are producers of functioning unconscious; I think our field is to be navigators without a compass and creators, together with the patient, of the unconscious.

Moreover, we can consider the tools by which this process is conducted today, and I say today because I hope that in twenty, fifty, a hundred years, things will be different. Today's tools are everything pertaining to the dreamlike, that is: the transformation that we do while awake of the sensory in images; the processes and activities of reverie; our capacity to dream the patient's communications, to deconstruct them, and to get from them a communicative meaning; and the construction, together with the patient, of worlds which, before that, were neither thinkable nor perhaps even existing. This toolkit helps us transform mental blocks into both thinkable thoughts and liveable emotions, and dream the unelaborated material that has transformed into symptom, making it thinkable, tolerable, and meaningful. An analyst transforms the stories that cannot be digested and weaves new sustainable meanings from the patient's mind. He is a co-narrator of the sensory that brings back the elaborated products to the realm of dreams and unconscious. He is a co-creator of the unconscious.

As I have said elsewhere, I think that, of all the roles that an analyst is called upon to play, he is above all a "magician" of sorts who uses the magic of sounds, of images, and of words. The analyst transforms internal reality, exorcises demons, rides dragons: he opens up a space for imagination, creativity, the absurd, and the unthought.

Tolstoy once told of how, as a child, he had built a train out of chairs with a friend, and was having a lot of fun with this game of make-believe, until his older brother came in and broke the spell by saying: "What a stupid game! Those are just chairs!"

This is the opposite of what an analyst is called upon to do: we should be able to see a train or a castle or anything else where there are only chairs; we should give life to stories and characters that do not yet exist. We are always co-narrators and never isolated authors, and we should always be aware that what we create together is meant to be replaced soon. The worlds that continually open up and close down during the session are known only to us and to the patient, who are their co-narrators.

> You do not know that magic and dragons were my passion before psychoanalysis, so you are handing me the next question on a plate. When and how does analysis become magic?

If someone called the firefighters to report a fire, it would be absurd if the fire brigade told him that the flames he sees are his unbridled emotions. Similarly, if a friend revealed to me that some of his skin moles seemed to be growing, obviously I would encourage him to consult a dermatologist. How would my mind work then if someone told me in session that he came to me because his moles are growing? For example, I could imagine a white blanket with holes on it. This white blanket could call to my mind a sheep with gashes in its wool fleece, through which one could see a blackness: the sheep is starting to look like a leopard. But if the patient in question kept talking about his fear of these growing moles, then maybe I could think of a blanket with bigger and bigger holes, revealing what lies underneath: perhaps it is a black panther.

So, from a starting point of a story about moles, the patient may find himself in a narrative that involves sheep, leopards, and black panthers!

Thus, in the consulting room we need a couch big enough for three characters: the sheep, the leopard, and the black panther, that keep fluctuating between themselves. There are no dragons, but I would say there was at least a bit of magic.

Of course, there is no direct match between moles and jungle stories: each analytic couple creates new and unexpected narratives, and it is crucial that one of the many dialogues that can be developed provides access to unknown and unconscious traits of the patient as well as ours.

While the firefighter's listening needs to be realistic, analytic listening in the consulting room needs a transformation process implemented by the "magic" filter of the analyst's ability to play and to dream in the session.

> Speaking about the identity of analysts, there are many colleagues who, when they suggest the names of other colleagues for a referral, name a man and a woman, rather than minding other aspects. We are quite far from the concept of the analyst as an interpreting function. In your opinion, how much does the analyst's gender, as opposed to other aspects, affect the stories that will be activated in analysis?

A lot, before the analysis begins. Nothing, after that.

I love it when I find an answer in two seconds.

I'm saying that at first fantasies, thoughts about a man or a woman, are lighted up. Once we get started, not at all. It matters what kind of person he or she is, indeed. It matters the type of person I meet, it matters the degree of mental health he has, the quality of the psychic functioning with that given patient.

> Let's start with one of the first problems each of us immediately stumbles across, and that for its urgency I would like to deal with before we talk about theories and everything else. What is the secret to avoid losing patients?

It amuses me a bit when I think that I claim to be not orthodox, but if certain things that Bion conceived continue to inspire in me a certain fascination and give complete answers, then I see no reason for not using them. In one of his seminars, Bion says that in each session we should always give the patient a good reason to come back the next time. In other words, the patient should play, have fun, enjoy it. It's like the *The Arabian Nights*, there has to be a Scheherazade[1] function able to always tell new stories, new tales, new metabolisations: a new game. It should be a game, that can be at times sad, at times happy, at times funny, at times tragic. I'm not saying "game" to diminish its emotional impact: a game can be a really serious thing. The patient should always receive from us a good reason to come the next day: this is how not to lose her. It means activating her curiosity, the pleasure of curiosity.

We have to ensure that the analysis can really be like *Star Trek*, the adventure series in which they land each time on unexpected and unknown worlds, curious to know new ones. Consider that analysis keeps expanding the world we explore: it can be a continuous expansion, as long as we do not cling to the already known. If we cling to the already known instead, we will find an example of castration anxiety, we will find Oedipus, we will find envy. We know it. That is a game we already played, we already saw. It's like roulette where you already know the number that will come out.

Note

1. Scheherazade, the protagonist of *The Arabian Nights*, is a beautiful and cunning girl. Upon learning that the king of Persia, in order to exact revenge for infidelity, decided to lay with a different slave each night, and then to kill her at dawn, Scheherazade resolved to put an end to the macabre ritual. Each night the girl tells a captivating tale to the king, interrupting it just before the sun rises. Ensnared by curiosity, the king postpones the execution to the next day, but the clever woman, as soon as she finishes a story, immediately begins another one, charming the king with her stories.

CHAPTER TWO

The rules of the game

While we are on the subject of games, the first thing you do when you begin playing is to establish some rules, without which the game is something else. So we start by fixing the rules that constitute our setting. The British once did five sessions a week. In Europe one generally travelled "by car", on four wheels. In France they have the tricycle …

… or the sidecar.

> Or the sidecar. New analysts and many therapists have, when things go well, a motor scooter, when things go badly a push scooter. On this subject, some say that anything less than three sessions per week is not analysis, because the method of free association loses its meaning in a low frequency relationship. Moreover you mentioned among the analyst's tools the deconstruction of actual speech; to what extent does doing this kind of transformation remain viable in a low frequency analysis—that we might even call psychoanalytic psychotherapy? These are situations in which external reality is knocking very loudly on the door.

This is a very complex question. I find that the metaphor you use is absolutely relevant; for my part, the sidecar can work; a motor scooter or bike can also work. If possible, I'd avoid the push scooter because it rather makes me think we are on one of those circus devices …

The unicycle?

The unicycle. Of course it is a lot harder to keep one's balance on a bike or unicycle. I would not let my grandmother, who could break a bone, sit on a one-legged chair. A chair with two legs would unsettle me too. So, a chair begins to be stable with three legs. More is better, when you can.

We can wonder whether it is absolute, mandatory. I think there are things which we must resign to. Water boils at 100 degrees Celsius. We can use any possible gimmick: of course by going up the Andes or somewhere else you can have water boil a few degrees earlier with an artifice, but you can't reinvent physics. Water boils at a certain temperature and I guess the same thing applies to nuclear fission: you need a certain critical mass to trigger a chain reaction. I believe that in analysis there needs to be a certain frequency in order to trigger a chain reaction. What exactly this frequency is no one can say, I think. As for my experience, I have always felt that with three or four sessions something begins to work differently, more lively, in a way that truly allows for a gradual forgoing of the aspects of reality, which are the ones we really have to forgo to be analysts.

Could you do an analytically oriented work with two sessions or even just one? Yes, obviously, but I would call it just that: an analytically oriented work. A person can be helped in his mental suffering even by meeting him once every fifteen days, or once a week. It is a legitimate work. However, this is not a job where there is an analysis, in the sense of being able to hand the patient, or the patient being able to develop, the tools he did not have beforehand and of which he then becomes the rightful owner. If we are talking about something that is profoundly transformative, I would say that the particle accelerator must be set to three to four sessions. Here I would say without excessive constraints, it can also be done with two sessions, on Monday and on Friday, it does not matter much. Today—I have no idea what our job will look like in 100 years—a certain frequency is unfortunately needed. Although you can still do a brilliant job, which helps suffering people, even once or twice a week. Yes, surely. However, we must resign ourselves to the fact that perhaps, without a high frequency, it will not be a full house renovation, of all the appliances in the house, of all the piping.

There used to be a distinction that I still hold basically valid. It may be that in this I am out of my time, but I find it useful to distinguish between psychoanalysis and psychotherapy, which has always played a lot, to be honest, on the number of sessions. Then obviously if you ask me whether I would prefer to do a five sessions analysis with an incompetent analyst or a two sessions analysis with Meltzer, I have no doubt that I would rather do a two sessions analysis with Meltzer, and I would call it analysis. If you ask me whether I would prefer to do one session a week with Ogden or five sessions with a proto-archaic-fundamentalist colleague, what you expect me to answer?

But here we are taking things to an extreme: if we are talking about an average well-functioning analyst, frequency is important. Frequency is important and is part of the constants that should be as fixed as possible, and that belong to the setting. So, we have the frequency, the duration of the session, the duration of the analysis in time, the relative stability—which is a key component, the rhythm. Rhythm is extremely important, especially for the most archaic nuclei that are present in each of us, the most primitive, that is to say autistic nuclei. We cannot get close to the most archaic nuclei—Bleger (1967) mentioned the agglutinated nucleus—with words; therapy happens through the rhythm, which is one of the most important aspects, related to the non-verbal, with projective identification, with other things well before the words.

You mention relative stability, rhythm, speaking of which I have a secret to disclose. You might not be aware of that, because teachers like you live in the attic of the analytic apartment building, but in the basement where young part-time analysts, who see maybe two patients a day or a week, dwell, the payment of skipped sessions is a place rife with bloody brawls or, even worse, sudden escapes with no return. Get down into the basement and tell us your opinion!

I'd say it's pretty simple, because it belongs to the "setting" chapter. One very important, but rarely discussed, thing in the "setting" chapter, is the constitution that we give ourselves. This also applies to playing a game of cards, when you say: "These are the rules we play by in the house. Want to play with me by these house rules or not?" The other person is free to accept or refuse. Likewise I think that, when I meet a patient, I share with him our constitution, which, once signed, applies to both of us. It is not a constitution made by me for the patients: our constitution is something to which I, too, am subjected. For this reason, if we establish our rules at the beginning of the analysis, they cannot then be disregarded. If I accept that a patient will not pay me the sessions he skips, how am I going to pay my house mortgage? How can I commit myself to paying my house mortgage, car loan payment, tuition fees for my children who go to university? So, why do I expect payment for the sessions that the patient misses? I do because I need it to live, there is no punitive or educational "So you won't skip sessions!" aspect.

If the patient skips sessions too often, this means that either he is foolish or the analysis is foolish. If an analyst manages to conduct a lively enough analysis, the patient should arrive ten minutes early because he can't wait to begin. Analysis is nice, this is what nobody understands. We keep talking about pain, suffering; the suffering of the analyst, the suffering of the patient. This liturgy of suffering is so monotonous, one ought at least to be able to have fun. If one has experienced a tragic event, obviously at that time he will not have anything to laugh at because, say, maybe his grandmother died. What I mean is that, even though grandmother died, at some point this fact can become like a sad story written by Blixen.[1] The transformation in narrative, in story, in something thinkable, is a step that makes us feel better compared to the brute event in itself, anyway. When we can turn any reality from brute event or source of brute sensoriality in a tale, maybe we wind up in Gadda's *Acquainted with Grief*,[2] but that is still better than feeling your head being hammered. So the pleasure of analysis means just that: being able to turn disoriented, disorganised, fragmented mental states into a story, which I sincerely hope will be as fun and adventurous as possible. Of course, every now and then one comes across Gadda too, and then we will cross Gadda's story too, but I repeat, and this is important, the pleasure of analysis should be exactly the same you feel in the playroom, or reading *The Arabian Nights*. The goal is to have fun too. What I am allergic to is all the emphasis on pain. Some amount of pain is necessary, it needs to be endured; if I'm taking antibiotics, I have to get an injection too, even though it hurts: it's not the end of the world. And if I realise that my antibiotics work, I'm going back to get a new jab tomorrow.

> From Freud to the present day, the duration of analysis became a lot longer—from a few months to several years—and some say it's too much.
> Should analysis be shorter or not?

I think that an analysis should last long enough. I do not think that there are objective end-of-analysis criteria regarding that; I realise that I'm taking a detour, but I'll give the answer in a roundabout way. There were once the famous criteria for ending an analysis, just as there were criteria for everything: there were, for instance, some well-known criteria for analysability. There was a well-marked trail, with plenty of road signs.

I really do not think that there are criteria for ending an analysis today; however, I have no doubt that in any analysis at some point will come, often completely unexpectedly, signals that it's almost time to end. Therefore, I believe that an analysis can end after a given time, when these signals point it out. On previous occasions I described what these signals might be, but it occurs to me that they usually might be the proof that the patient has a toolkit good enough to get by.

> However, maybe the problem concerning the duration of our therapies is felt more sharply today than in the past. Contemporary patients, in part for socio-economic reasons, in part for inner resistances, are rather reluctant to undergo long-term dependency relationships. Stefano Bolognini claims that today's children have a hard time experiencing constant and reliable long-time care. Families break down and are recomposed, caregivers alternate between parents, grandparents, babysitters, sports coaches, and teachers. The result tends to be a lower confidence in entrusting oneself to another.
>
> So, how can we deal with this mistrust towards dependence, when we suggest an analytical work that takes up so much time during the week and that can often last for many years?

To begin with, I am absolutely convinced that we should always keep transience in mind: it is not a given that psychoanalysis will last for ever and ever, or that people should necessarily do analysis. I think that analysis should be made by those who want to do it and by those who experience that doing analysis makes them feel better the next day, the next week, and so on. I imagine that at some point it should be some kind of standing appointment, like friends who see each other on Mondays, Wednesdays, and Fridays to play a game of cards. Analysis should be something nice, analysis should be something fun, analysis should be something that looks like a game. It should be something you enjoy and for which you are willing to commit energy, time, and money, like when you go to see a sports match. What if you do not want to go see a match between Inter and AC Milan, because you are not interested in soccer? You are free not to go: it should be a pleasure, not something mandatory.

Maybe you have to find out that, if you suffer from a phobia, an inhibition, panic attacks, or any other disorder, certainly you can fix emergency situations or particularly serious ones with drugs or other means, but if you want to get out of it for real, so far the only known way is, unfortunately, psychoanalysis. This psychoanalysis of ours suffers a strange fate, because there are times when it seems that it can heal everything, and times when whole areas of mental suffering, that allegedly absolutely no longer belong among things that it can take care of, are being removed from it. It's clear to say what we're talking about.[3]

You mentioned going to see a match: do you not know how much stadium tickets cost nowadays? Let's talk about money then, one of the taboos that has replaced sex since more puritan times. Some young therapists feel rather embarrassed about getting paid. Certainly there is some difficulty in acknowledging the value of one's work, but it seems to me that there is also an idea, rather widespread among new analysts, according to which analysis should be a right for everybody, more so in as difficult a period as we are going through.

Argentina, where it was said that even taxi drivers picking you up at the airport had done analysis, comes to mind. I'm talking about a kind of social responsibility of the analyst. And then there's the crisis, and there's the fact that some patients are really struggling to make ends meet. So, I would like to examine in greater depth the relationship between money, inner fantasies—both of the patient and the analyst—and external reality.

Let me tell you a couple of things. First of all, I find that it is absolutely untrue that the analyst asks for payment because it is symbolically important, and so on. If I were rich, I think I would not ask for payment for analysis because I enjoy it, I like it, I heal myself. I get so many advantages out of that; I really need analysis! Consider that the analyst depends on analysis much more than the patient. The patient is satisfied with three or four sessions a week. The analyst needs thirty-two sessions a week, so he is much more addicted; paradoxically, he needs it much more than others. So, honestly, if I were rich I think I wouldn't even ask for a symbolic dollar in payment: there is no need of this symbolism of restitution. The patient will give me something back with his warm smile, his handshake, his gratitude, if and when he comes.

So, why do I ask for payment? I would say that I ask for payment, that the analyst in general asks for payment for the work he gives up in order to be an analyst. If I did not get paid when I act as an analyst, in order to support myself I would have to work as a neurologist, that is the job I was doing before, at least for a few hours a day; so I ask for payment for giving up work as a neurologist. That is, the patient does not pay me for what happens in the session, he pays me so that I can support myself, to be able to give something to the grocer and the butcher. Having no money of my own, not having a trade, not having a firm, I have to worry about earning money to give to the butcher or to the baker. Hence the money I have to ask the patient, because analysis is a luxury we cannot afford to do for free.

Since you like *Star Trek*, let's take our spaceship and go into a dimension where there is an alter ego of Dr Ferro who comes from a rich family. Thankfully I am not a patient of yours in that world, since I am wondering what kind of smiles and handshakes I would have to give you to compensate for some of what you give me. Isn't that so?

THE RULES OF THE GAME 19

One might even disclose the secret that, at times, the patient also heals the analyst. I am not saying there is a mutual analysis, but I have little doubt that from a mental point of view the analyst benefits from the number of hours of analysis he does.

> I really have to extort this secret from you, then: what good is analysis for the analyst?

Well, it would be like asking, in a world full of bacteria, what good is antibiotic for the doctor. I believe that doing many hours of analysis is good for the maintenance and continued development of the tools for thinking, that it keeps them in top shape, whereas over time there might be malfunctions.

So we can ask ourselves: what is good for the analyst to maintain his mental life sufficiently alive? I would say a few hours in which he is not acting as an analyst, in which he does something else, in which he lives. Consider an analyst who lives his whole life in a room.

The analyst has to live, has to be a human being who lives his experiences; having a second job would be ideal, but usually there is no time for that. I would like an analyst who had a fish shop, a butcher shop, or an analyst who works as a dermatologist, a palaeontologist. Who does something else too, like the old analysts, the old generations, did sometimes.

Apart from this, it is crucial to have a few hours in which to do nothing, leaving the mind fallow for a bit; doing nothing is an art.

And then we go back to the hours of treatment, because every patient we treat is always a little-known plot to explore: analysis done to someone is always a form of self-analysis.

Finally, I think that the analyst should cultivate anything he likes: or course reading, watching movies, or various artistic activities, but also just living, dealing with the normal things that everyone does, arguing with his girlfriend, making peace, going to the movies, living.

Could it be said that the most common disease of analysts is depression, and that many of them are being cured by their patients, or not?

Why couldn't we say it? It's true, there are analysts that feel ill without patients, who really have an addiction to patients, who feel well thanks to having patients. I think that an analyst should have a sufficiently healthy life to say: "I would be fine, I would relish winning three million dollars in the lottery and not having to work anymore." No, no, no, I do not like that one has to depend on patients, that there needs to be someone else who is ill in order for him to be well.

Second, I believe that the analyst should have—within the limits of the human and the possible—a sufficiently satisfactory life. And if I may say it, sexually satisfying too, because otherwise trouble is bound to happen. You should be generally satisfied with your life, even of going on a holiday and of being happy about it. The analyst should be glad if a patient skips the session, glad of being able to do something else, to go get some ice cream or buy a book. And he should not feel bad if there are no patients, this is unacceptable.

You said that analysis is the antibiotic that is also beneficial to the analyst: just like every drug it's got to have side effects as well, right? What are the main ones?

The major side effect is what happened to me when a friend told me that her husband at that time had a low level of plasmatic iron, and I thought she wanted to tell me it had been a long time since I had paid him a visit, so his "iron level"[4] was low. The risk is to be always locked in an analytic mode: if a friend, while having dinner with us, tells us that the night before he ate at a terrible restaurant, maybe we think that he's complaining about how we made the risotto. I think the major risk is the excess of interpretation, it is that the analyst at some point will come to believe he can interpret the world, reality, the future, while he can only interpret what happens in psychoanalytic therapy.

When I was a candidate, I once witnessed a dispute between two training analysts, of different orientations, watching together the white thigh of the horse painted by Paolo Uccello.[5] One claimed that the horse's thigh, the gluteus, could be nothing but a breast: so white and round it was that it could only represent the breast, while the other retorted, "No, look, it's so muscular it can only refer to the penis!" I was listening and was left quite puzzled. I do not like applied psychoanalysis; I believe it can be applied to the patient and nothing else, at most to ourselves or to the analytic couple. I do not believe that psychoanalysis can be applied to anything outside psychoanalytic therapy at all. Besides that, let's have fun, why not? If one wants to apply it to trigonometry or the interpretation of a work of art, nothing wrong with that, but there's that famous joke about the Mona Lisa's smile that might be either the smile of a woman who learned she was pregnant or the smile of a woman who learned she was *not* pregnant.

I mean, psychoanalysis has a specific field: healing mental suffering. The purpose of the scalpel is to cut the belly of the patient, but can we use a scalpel to cut a piece of paper? Of course! It is not the use it was made for, but nobody is stopping us. Just remember then that using the same scalpel on somebody's belly on the street is a crime!

Where there is money, of course, here come taxes. Which is a thorny issue, since, in some countries in the world, analysts too are struggling to pay their taxes. I touched on the subject three times in public: the first time I got a standing ovation from my colleagues, the second time I was told that this subject was not to be discussed, the third time, the funniest one, an influential colleague replied that anybody can pay as much tax as it takes to make their

superego satisfied. Care to give me your opinion or shall we move
on to the next question right away?

I think it's something absolutely specific to each person as a
human being according to which social reality he lives in. The
world in which I would like to live is a world where everybody
pays their taxes according to what they earn, be they analysts,
be they barbers, be they butchers. I would see no reason why
an analyst ought to have less of an obligation compared to a
barber, or more of an obligation either. If a barber does not
pay his taxes, you cannot say that his duties are different from
those of a podiatrist, even though one takes care of the head
while the other takes care of the feet.

Being an analyst is a job like any other, like being a painter,
so I think that analysts should pay their taxes like everybody
else. If someone finds himself in circumstances where paying
all his taxes would leave him starving, his common sense will
tell him to evade that twenty per cent that would allow him to
eat; but if he can pay them all, that would be better for everyone. That is, this does not seem a category for which there is
a special rule, so that paying taxes would have a symbolic,
special, different meaning for analysts. You pay taxes because
there are law enforcement agencies, there is a revenue service,
and you as an Italian or Czech citizen are expected to do so, to
contribute to the community's functioning too.

I would certainly love to pay taxes as they pay them in
Finland, where everybody pays them dearly and pays them
all, but there is free analysis as long as you need it, for years on
end. I was once invited to dinner by five or six Scandinavian
colleagues, and I signed to each of them a piece of paper,
because they were splitting the cost of my dinner between the
six of them; my signature was enough to assure that indeed
one-sixth of my dinner was paid by each of them.

No, it does not seem to me that analysts are a category that
needs to be protected, nor vilified, and then I would not bring

superego into the picture while talking about taxes; you pay your taxes because you have to.

Notes

1. Karen Blixen, famous twentieth-century Danish writer, author of several short stories and novels, the most famous of which is *Out of Africa*.
2. Translator's note: Often described as a roman-à-clef, Carlo Emilio Gadda's *Acquainted with Grief* is an unfinished novel that references events from Gadda's life and places he lived in, while being ostensibly set in a fictional foreign nation and populated with fictional characters.
3. This issue was raised by the publication of the Italian National Institute of Health guidelines on the treatment of autistic children on January 26, 2012, which promote rehabilitation interventions to the detriment of psychotherapy. As a result, in several countries, including France and Italy, a heated debate on the relationship between psychoanalysis and autism was sparked.
4. Translator's note: The family name Ferro translates as "Iron".
5. Paolo Uccello was an Italian painter of the fifteenth century.

CHAPTER THREE

Beginnings

A nd now let us leave the accountant to get back to the office and meet our patient for the first time. The first interview. At the start of training it was quite clear to me that the consultation interviews were the easiest part of the job. In Italy, psychologists that are not specialised psychotherapists can legally do them, and oftentimes interns and trainees do the first interviews in public healthcare. Even in the analytic literature that I studied the books talk about an initial phase, which should be short enough, that comes before the transference neurosis.

Do we still believe in transference neurosis?

I'm just telling you what I read: *relata refero!*[1] And here I thought this was going to be the easy part, while the stormy one was supposed to come later. By dint of losing patients I learned first-hand that the first interview is actually central. And I think that, in particular, analysis with teenagers helped us to leave behind the idea of these two, maximum three interviews, and to take our time, at last achieving in due time the construction of the setting. How could we rethink these first interviews? The part that comes before the constitution, the construction of the constitution.

I think it's like when there's a first romantic encounter: how does it happen?

There is love at first sight and there are couples that see each other and go straight for the couch, then there are those who take two years just to sit on the same bench. I do not think you can make generalisations. Surely the first encounter is extremely important because if we manage to avoid polluting it with questions, if we avoid asking about childhood, if we avoid asking things that do not really interest us, we can provide enough frameworks on which the patient may be able to stage the things he wants to talk about and especially those he does not want to talk about; that is a good way to start.

What about case history?

Case history has nothing to do with psychoanalysis, because if we consider that the whole analysis is based on what we build together, thinking that there is a significant case history is in itself a folly. You can do your own case history, it has no psychoanalytic relevance, it has a psychiatric relevance, or it might interest somebody who works in a psychiatric service and needs to file a case history because, if the police come, the fact that this guy tried to kill his sister has to be in the papers. However, if you are an analyst, in your office, what do you need a case history for? The history is a way to gag a patient, it is a way to ensure that those things that make him feel ill do not come out. Ogden stated brilliantly that we have to be able to dream with the patient those things that, undreamed, have become symptoms. Do we need to have read Freud to understand this though? It may be that before achieving this elementary simplicity poor Ogden had to read Freud or maybe Ogden's analyst had to read Freud, and then maybe Ogden had to read Winnicott. However, when Ogden tells us this, do we need to start again from the Rat Man case or can we start from this situation that Ogden tells us and move on from there? Why should we waste our time? It's so elementary, we have to transform into dream that which, not transformed enough, had become symptom: we must transform the symptom into dream.

So analysis is the place dedicated to the dream, and the couch was chosen from the beginning as a place halfway between wakefulness and sleep, between dream and reality. Speaking of which let me tell you a little anecdote: a patient of mine, who is a student at a psychotherapy school, tells his teacher that he chose to carry out his compulsory therapy with an analyst and that he lies on the couch, and the teacher's reply petrifies him: "But the couch is unfashionable!" The first question I ask you is almost rhetorical: is the couch really unfashionable? The second question, which is perhaps less rhetorical, regards those colleagues who often use the "unicycle". When I was in training they said using the couch for therapies once or twice a week could be dangerous because the patient tends to regress, and containing him may be hard. What do you think?

I would say: let's try and see!

Had I to give a suggestion to my grandchild, I would tell him that analysis does not depend on where one lies down, analysis depends on how two people mentally work together. So, just as being on the couch does not give the status of analysis, likewise not being on the couch does not take away the status of analysis. I have had patients in the weirdest places: I do not think I've ever written, but I have told, about a patient who did not want to lie down on the couch and with whom we had a long period of analysis. We met each other four sessions a week, face to face, because she was too haunted by the idea of not being able to control the situation, my reactions, the emotions I might have. After some time, I told her: "Look, I grow tired of being like this, staring at each other for fifty minutes straight, if you do not mind I am going to turn around." And then I turned around on my office chair—a swivel chair with wheels—so the patient came in, sat down, and I turned around. We went on for another six months of analysis with me turning my back and feeling a bit relaxed. After which the patient began to talk about the fact she had to make a move, it was time to make this move, and she wanted a more comfortable house. It seemed clear that the patient was saying that there had to be a move in our analysis. When the day we had agreed on for the "move" came, obviously I was expecting the patient to move to the couch so that I could go back to my armchair, instead the patient came in and sat down in my armchair. I could have done a thousand different things there, give seven thousand interpretations of all kinds; without a moment's hesitation, I went to lie down on the couch, and so we did about six months of analysis with the patient behind me in my armchair and me lying down on the couch. I repeatedly warned the patient she did not know what she was missing, because lying down on the couch was much more comfortable, and after six months the patient had a dream in which her secretary was arbitrarily occupying a place that she was entitled to. Within a few weeks there was talk of another move and at last this was the final one. I finally went back to my armchair and the patient lay down on the couch. It took at least three years to do this turn, but it was an analysis in all respects, a very normal analysis. What matters is knowing how to play.

For this reason I would like to formalise—even though not everyone agrees, and so I do not know if it will happen—that there is no difference between the analysis of adults, children, and adolescents. Indeed, we can learn to see in children the infantile aspects that are within us and within patients. From adults we can learn to see the most structured aspects. Clearly, a children's analyst will be much less worried about a possible infraction of the setting by the patient, because he will not perceive it as an attack at all, but rather as a mode of communication, and above all as a game. Together we can play with anything, there is not one thing we can not play with. And thus play it down.

The analyst will have to ask himself why this happens, and what does it mean: obviously the analyst should possess a mind able to think and to question what's going on, and to try to produce a meaning that might be expressed or not; what use to make then of what one has realised depends on countless variables.

It seems that Freud chose to sit behind the patient's couch because he could not stand a whole day of stares. So, perhaps the couch is also convenient to the analyst, is it not?[2]

I have no doubt, I believe that having the patient on the couch is what works best, as well as the most convenient situation for the analyst! Indeed, Freud had the idea of the couch because he could not bear to be looked at by patients all day. The couch, thanks to which there is no face to face interaction, allows the patient to let his mind wander, so that thoughts and fantasies may float. The same is true of the analyst, who can set aside reality and more easily access a world of fantasy, of association, of mental routes, of narratives, free from the impact with reality.

All in all, I do not think that using the couch is crucial in analysis, which I think can be carried on in many different positions. Obviously, it is always important to ask oneself why a patient prefers to be in one position rather than in another. For instance, it is very difficult for patients with severe mental suffering to lie on the couch, because in doing so their mind wanders a bit too far from reality, in worlds that are often persecutory. I recall a patient who once told me he had a dream in which there was a lion behind him, ready to pounce on him at any moment.

Another patient, after finally agreeing to lie down on the couch, dreamed she was in a cradle made of sharp blades that cut her and made her bleed. So, I do not think that lying down on the couch and beginning a *Star Trek*-like journey to unknown universes is easy for everybody. There are patients who need to begin their journey on the couch and not aboard the Enterprise, visiting the outskirts of their city before exploring other cities, or maybe visiting other worlds or galaxies.

So, as I said, it is common to find patients who do not want to lie on the couch, and it is possible to work with them face to face in a variety of situations.

> There is a certain ritual of the session: generally the patient has the right to start the session and as Luciana Nissim (2001) said, he gets the honour of the last word. Isn't that so?

Well, basically I would say yes, generally I would let the patient begin unless he keeps quiet for more than five minutes. It is not a matter of respecting the setting or of an idea, there is no idea like, after five minutes the patient is going to feel lonely, behind it; no! It's just that I get bored, that is, in order to function and play, in order to work and dream, after a while I need some contact.

> So there is an underlying idea, the idea that after five minutes the couple breaks up.

Yes.

> Because the analytic function of the couple, in the person of the analyst Ferro, needs contact.

On a warm day you can lie in bed with your girlfriend, but, after ten minutes in bed, I will reach for her! But if she's asleep, I'll let her sleep.

There is a contact function, in my opinion, that is, one has to keep contact to do things. So generally I wait for the patient to begin the session, then the fifth or fourth minute in—which should be even sooner I think—the third minute in I say, "So?" or, "What's up today?"; "Why so quiet?" Some nonsense, some dumb silly line.

I do not know about the last word, I never considered the issue of who had the right to the last word. However, I usually tell him, "See you next time." Yes, I let him end with his speech.

What I mean is that maybe it is not appropriate to make an interpretation or comment in closing the session.

No, no, I would not daze him with talk right before he leaves, poor thing, no. I always leave myself some time to see how he reacts. Something that is still important to me in the field is what happens after I enter the scene.

We are talking about internal and external frames, so I ask you a seemingly trivial question. At the time of my training the rule was that the analyst had to have a desk phone and an answering machine. Those who, like me, are "nomads", do not even think about it anymore, besides texts are replacing voice calls, a bit out of ease of use, a bit because they feel less intrusive, maybe. Moreover, a considerable number of patients search for therapists on the internet and even resort to email for introductions: "Dear Doctor, I have anxiety. Can we meet?"

Can we talk of a fracturing of the field or of a pre-field and of the transition from a "I'm here/I'm not here" swing to a more digital "I'm here a bit/I'm starting to be here" that dilutes the dichotomy between presence and absence?

If you, like some friends of mine, have a son living in Sweden, or like some others in Singapore, then it is normal to see him several times a week via Skype. I do not see why it should be any different for the analyst. Once there was the phone and that was it, but now many communications happen via texting. I believe that there is an unchanging part of the setting, certain basic structures, and then a culturally variable part. If in a hundred years we will have holograms of ourselves that we will be able to send around, we will do analysis via hologram; where's the problem?

If a patient texts me saying that he will come fifteen minutes late, I reply: "OK." Certainly I do not hold long discussions via text, I do not do interpretations over the telephone, but I can reply him, "OK." Or, if someone contacts me for the first time by email, I reply: "Dear Sir, would you please call me after 9 pm from Monday to Thursday?" This is not a sin, if you use logic and innocence; I would not be an overly concerned analyst that sees everything as a sin. "Omnia munda mundis!" Father Cristoforo[3] would say: everything is pure to the pure!

> Speaking of sins, I have another one to submit for your attention. For some time I have been doing a lot of public speaking, so I get seen more often than before, even by some patients. Moreover, in a small town like Modena or Pavia after a while everybody gets acquainted with everybody else, so I have been thinking this: if the analyst is no longer a mirror, but a co-builder of stories, can we think that the absolute need for confidentiality with respect to getting acquainted or to associating outside the analysis becomes less pressing? I am not talking about cancelling any privacy, but can it be that getting a bit acquainted promotes some stories rather than some others, without disrupting work? Or is there more?

Let's see what we mean by acquaintance. Obviously I would discourage a young colleague from going lap dancing at the weekend, generally, at least not in the city where he lives. Regarding meeting someone in the town square or sitting at the same café while you are having a drink, or meeting the patient at the bookstore and exchanging a "hello" or "good evening", I do not see those as sinful contacts, those are random encounters in a small town. It depends on what kind of acquaintance we are speaking of. If you belong to the same tennis club, where there are ten thousand members, where's the problem? Or if you meet in the town square or while having coffee. Of course, more frequent relationships, above a certain limit, can restrict the stories that can be created, they promote overly real stories; thus they pollute the field, preventing the initial totipotent narrative. If one rode through Pavia on horseback, playing a trumpet, he would be either crazy, or he would come to be identified as the trumpeter rider, and then he would be too distinctive. Of course, when it comes to holding public office—if one is an analyst and at the same time the local police commander—one will do what he can. *Cum grano salis*.[4] Common sense and honesty are the touchstones: it's better not to assume that behind every new or strange thing there is a sin or an infraction of the setting or who knows what else, but at the same time it's better to retain some discretion, in the sense of allowing the development of as many stories as possible.

> We keep talking about sins. I have to question you on one of the foundations underpinning psychoanalysis: in analysis one talks and does not act. And whoever does act usually is ambivalent about it.
>
> Then interpersonal relationship came into the mix, and then Thomas Ogden came and made a mess with his interpretive actions (1994) and others still, like Bolognini's interpret-action (2008). Now someone is talking about variable setting, action suited to "that" patient, and now I find Ferro doing analysis while lying on the couch …

Just once in my lifetime!

... once in your lifetime. So the discretion of analysts obviously takes on a very different role. Now I'm asking you: to what extent can you act in an analysis and what are the boundaries to keep in mind?

I would say: maximum freedom of action for the patient, minimum freedom of action for the analyst. The patient may act as he wishes: thankfully the patient does not know that he can bring some toys from home and sit on the floor playing with them; an adult patient does not usually do this, but he could. I do not see what an analyst of adult patients might have to object to if a patient brought some toy soldiers with him and wanted to play with them: it is his right to do so. We would not tell him: "No, you can not play!" That's his game, his dream, his mode of communication. Or the patient might come up with some clean sheets of paper, draw a few nice pictures, and communicate with them. Certainly so.

However, thankfully, the patient does not know that, because lying down on the armchair without the patient looking at us, is much more comfortable to us than having to sit on the floor or at the desk looking at his drawings. It would be much more tiring. So a patient has the freedom to express himself, within reasonable limits of course. I give maximum freedom of action to a patient, if he wants to have a session under the table, maybe I would tell him "Woof" because he is acting like a dog in a kennel, or the next day we would pretend being in the Seven Dwarfs' cottage. No idea, depends on what arises. So, I believe that the analyst does not have this freedom, I believe that the analyst's freedom to act should absolutely be keep in check, avoiding excesses. Interpretive action is different from other types of act one can do, but I cannot help but wonder why. I would be very careful that it is not a short-cut. I would keep the analyst firmly sitting in his chair, with a minimum of action, according to common sense. I recall one of the few cases in which I and Eugenio Gaburri dismissed a candidate during the final exam of training. The case began with the story of a pregnant patient who, walking into the consulting room, had stumbled and fallen to the ground, and the candidate wrote: "Of course I stood motionless and did not touch the patient."

Oh no, a pregnant woman, or not pregnant for that matter, falls in a heap right before your eyes, and you do not help her? I mean that this is nonsense, it is not analytic neutrality. The analyst should be contained, and ask himself why is he doing an act, or an action, and whether it is safe to do it. But if a patient is throwing himself out of the window, you catch him by his feet, of course, or if a patient stumbles, you help him up, or if a patient has the warning signs of a heart attack, you turn off the setting and call an ambulance.

This idea of turning off and on the setting seems very interesting to me: it helps us distinguish between two different modes of operation of the analyst. If we leave aside external reality, then we can take it "seriously" again when we need to.

Yes, but when we take seriously reality, just before that we turn off the setting. Reality can only come in when the setting is turned off. If there was an earthquake, it would be foolish to just stand there and try to interpret the shock that the child felt as he broke away from the nipple of the mother—it would be absurd in any event to say such a thing even without the earthquake—but let's imagine there is an earthquake: what do we say to the patient, what do we do? We wait and, if there is a second tremor, we get out. At that time though we turn off the setting, we are no longer analyst and patient, we are two frightened individuals who have to get safely out of that room.

It is true however that many times patients recall as an important part of therapy those rare instances when the analyst took care of them in some other, more tangible way. Obviously it is not something you can do routinely, let's say it is an uncommon device.

If a patient walks in with a nosebleed what do we do, do we not hand him a handkerchief, a towel?

A bit like saying, let's turn off the setting but let's not turn off ourselves!

Yes, we should not turn off the patient. Do you deny a towel to a patient who comes in completely soaked in winter? Those are things that have to do with common sense; I would never leave common sense and good manners out of the consulting room.

A patient tells me that he's cold. Do I interpret the distance he feels between us or do I turn on the heater?

If I have one, I turn on the heater, no doubt there. What I am thinking then is a different matter, of course, things do not stop there. If we are in the consulting room, why should I not turn on the heater, if I have it and I use it? Of course, I would wonder why the patient told me he wants the heater on today at half past two but not yesterday, what is he talking about, whether he is telling me that he is tired, whether he is telling me that he is feeling ill, whether he is telling me that he is feeling cold. I would not say all these things to him, poor thing, I'd try to understand: what does he want to tell me with this request?

A patient tells me: "I'm dying of thirst!" Imagine if I replied: "Are you telling me that since you didn't meet me for several days, the session is like an oasis, and you crossed the long desert of the weekend, so you are dehydrated?" I would give him a glass of water without much of a fuss, and then with time and reflection we will understand why it happened.

There is a Sicilian slang idiom, that might be unsuitable for a book. Translated, it would be "touching your bottom with your shirt". If Maria is touching her bottom with her shirt it means that she can not touch it with her hands, that she has to do everything with white gloves, that she is unable to get into intimacy, that she always need distance. I do not think that the analyst should "touch his bottom with his shirt", that he should have a phobia of contact. He should have neither a phobia of emotional contact nor a phobia of physical contact. If a patient at the end of analysis gives you a kiss on the cheek, you just take it and smile; I would definitely avoid phobic aspects.

Notes

1. Latin: "I tell what I have been told" (Herodotus).
2. The material of this and a few other questions is taken from the interview, "Global Perspectives: an Interview with Antonino Ferro", by Jill Choder-Goldman, LCSW, being published in the journal *Psychoanalytic Perspectives*.
3. A character from Alessandro Manzoni's *The Betrothed*.
4. Latin: With a grain of salt; with a bit of common sense and scepticism.

CHAPTER FOUR

Matters of theory

We are talking about the relationship between analytic neutrality and what I would call analytic naturalness. In classical theory, the analyst traditionally acts neutrally, like a mirror in which the patient can see himself reflected with his transferential demands, projections, conflicts. That being the case, anything we add, our metaphors, our acts of encouragement, our very person, becomes an extra variable that jeopardises the balance of the system, an expropriation of sorts of the patient's space. Things have changed radically since the coming of various relational models. Now, what merit can we give to analytic neutrality, and how can we rethink analytic neutrality so that it remains a useful tool as opposed to something obsolete?

I just find the concept of analytic neutrality ridiculous. It would be like envisioning self-fertilisation. It's like saying that we want to conceive a child just by making eye contact. No, you have to "get dirty" elsewhere. I find that the idea of two people being together in a neutral way is ridiculous, it's just impossible. If we envision the mirror-analyst, it's like having a mirror blocking the entrance to a garage; you drive there to park your car inside it, but where are you supposed to park your car, if there is no space beyond the mirror?

The patient feels a need for accommodation, for a mind capable of containing him. An analyst has to let himself be penetrated by the patient's anxieties, by his emotions. In order to be penetrated he needs to be hollow; how are you supposed to get into a mirror? Maybe just in Alice's story.[1]

And then, there being two people, I believe that neutrality is impossible, since the very instant there are two people something is being co-built together. And an analyst in grey, a neutral analyst, contributes to a weave in which there is grey yarn. If the analyst wears a red or blue sweater, something more lively, where there is also red and blue, will be woven instead. That neutrality is not a colour, that grey is not a colour, that's wishful thinking. In the game of weaving with the patient, that is, the analyst in grey makes the patient's yarn intertwine with his own grey yarn.

> I suspected that the classic textbook definition of neutrality would not satisfy you. If I have to think about the way I understand it, that has been useful to me so far but that I'm also pondering about currently, it is neutrality with respect to the patient's varying needs. I mean that with the patient one is neutral within intrapsychic conflict, or in the patient's game of relations. Whether the patient stays with his wife or they separate, for example, is an issue that I'm neutral on, because I really do not know what's better for the patient; in this regard too, however, I wonder whether it is actually true that the analyst is or has to be neutral, I'm not sure.

Who is the wife in session, though?

> I could see that one coming.

We would be overly practical analysts if during a session we were to think about concrete facts. It's one thing if you meet your friend Marco, who tells you that he does not know whether he and Louise should break up. Then he tells you that Louise did this and that, and you decide that Louise is not trustworthy, or you tell him that he's being unfair to Louise instead; we are there in a mood where we talk about concrete, actual facts between people.

When the analytic apparatus is activated because there is a tool, the setting, it's like being at the theatre and the lights go out, the voices fall silent, and from that moment on you only hear whispers: then begins the session. When the session begins, the patient's wife is no longer the patient's wife, she is a character in the field, and through that character who knows who the patient is talking about? About parts of the analyst that the patient feels rejected by, about parts of the analyst that he loathes, about aspects of himself that he calls "my wife" because he cannot recognise them as his own. When the psychoanalytic setting is activated we are no longer dealing with people, we are dealing with characters, so the patient's wife will be anything except the patient's actual wife.

And obviously we do not know who this wife is. Let's say a patient complains: "My wife is violent, keeps losing her temper, is irritable." It seems pretty obvious that he's talking about an incontinent aspect, which might be the analyst's, or perhaps the patient's: nevertheless in the field. So we have to deal with this incontinent aspect: is it something that he will be able to integrate?[2]

However, consider that a patient never speaks only about his external reality. A patient tells me he suffers from premature ejaculation. He is not actually talking about premature ejaculation with me, I do not care a bit about his sexual affairs, he is telling me instead that he is not able to contain his emotions, that they escape him. Or conversely, if a patient told me about delayed ejaculation, should I be concerned with his performance under the sheets? The problem he is talking about is that he can not let himself go, that he's always living in a state of hyper-continence. So I will be interested in seeing some of this hyper-continence in the field: how does he narrate it, besides delayed ejaculation? And what can we do to loosen this hyper-continence which is one of the facets of being obsessive?

The story always becomes different from the one that was narrated. And we have to go towards what we do not know. Only by going towards what we do not know, we understand more about this delayed ejaculation. If it appears that he would like to kill his grandmother in order to get her inheritance, then we will begin to make a film in which he's afraid of these murderous impulses, which he holds back, and then he will most likely heal even from the stated symptom. But the symptom is how someone presents himself; obviously the issue is never the symptom, which is the emergence of something as yet unknown.

> If we think that there are characters in place of people, then the problem of the analyst's self-disclosure takes on a different meaning too. If there is something I realised over the years about this subject, it is that as much as they look intrigued by our life, patients have no genuine desire to know our business. Rather, they want to know if we can understand them. Maybe they want to know if we could play a certain character, if they are able to couple with the character that we are at that time on the scene. That being the case, can we consider self-disclosure as communicating to the patient the result of our mental coupling, an unveiling of our thoughts, of emotions, of reverie?

I'd say that's one way of casting the characters that is needed at that time to move the story onward. Indeed self-disclosure, meant as a veritable story of our business, could be made up of whole cloth, it need not necessarily correspond to an actual fact from the analyst's life. It can be completely fabricated. Let's say a patient is afraid that the analyst might be too fragile, and describes a terrible dog that he is afraid of. The analyst might say: "You know, as a child the story that I found most thrilling was *The Hound of the Baskervilles*." Meaning that I'm used to dealing with dogs. Or he might say: "Oh, I'm sure it's a nice dog, as a child I was lucky enough to live in a home where my father kept two Dobermanns, three Neapolitan mastiffs and two pit bulls." It's all made up, but it's useful to tell the patient, "Look, your dog really does not scare me!" I do not know, is that clear? It really becomes another thing altogether. It's a dream in session, a dream co-construction of the session.

> So, let's talk about what is true or not true. When collecting questions to ask you, I thought about a patient who was convinced that one time, months before, I had told him a lie in order to cancel a session. Or about a colleague of mine that recently told me that she had cried after a very intense interview. Afterwards the patient, on seeing her looking flushed, asked her if she had a cold. The colleague replied that it was just a bit of an allergy. Here, given what you just told me, I would ask you about the relationship between lie, falsehood, and self-disclosure. Because until now I thought that, if the analyst tells a lie, he somehow breaks a pact of honesty. However, one needs to understand what it means to say that the analyst is telling a lie; perhaps he is telling a story?

I would start from a popular Sicilian proverb: *U fuiri è virgogna ma è savvamentu 'i vita*, which translated means that fleeing is shameful but sometimes necessary to save your life. I remember once, when I was working in a public service for the drug addicted, and there was a brawl for methadone, there was a huge mess. Back home—I was living alone in an apartment at the end of a long corridor, on the top floor—I heard knocking at the door, I went to open it, and there were some shady characters who asked me if Dr Ferro was at home. Meanwhile these guys were openly *talking* about a beating, and thankfully I said: "No, you see, Dr Ferro went out: he went to Corso Garibaldi to play table football!"

Besides, I never played table football in my life, and so this story tells us something else: that a lie as opposed to the truth is always adorned. While the truth is bare. "Today I saw you in your car, driving through Corso Garibaldi." If one wasn't there, maybe he just says that he was in Viale Magenta instead. But if he actually was there, but wasn't supposed to, because maybe there lives his ex-girlfriend, he blurts out that he was in Viale Magenta, aboard a number 32 bus, when he saw his aunt Peppina that he had not seen in years, and there was this policeman with a full black beard; that is, the lie is very adorned.

Back to the point though: are we allowed to lie? Sure we are, thank goodness we are. As Bion says, the lie requires a thinker. The lie opens up a world, creates it. Think of a child who steals jam, and is asked the fateful question: "Did you steal the jam?" If your grandmother is so foolish that she would beat you up if you stole the jam, it wouldn't be very clever to admit it. The lie allows you to live in worlds that are perhaps less violent, less persecutory. If a woman has a jealous husband who would beat her if she went to a lingerie store, she will say she only went to the grocery store. Looks like self-defence to me.

The lie is a defence just like any other defences we enact. When we use an excitatory, manic, avoidant, omnipotent defence, or any other defence, we use a form of lie with regard to something that we cannot bear. As long as we cannot bear that thing, we use the lie as a defence. When we will no longer be afraid of that thing there will be no more reason to hide ourselves behind a lie.

Speaking of defence, recently, as I was walking down the street, I was fiddling a bit with some ideas to put into this book; then I happened to think about defence mechanisms. I asked myself: "Defending against what?" We defended ourselves against anxiety …

… Unbearable.

Exactly. So I wondered if in a metaphorical system different from the military one, made of resistance and attacks on linking …

Is anybody still using that stuff?

Apparently so. While perhaps psychic defences could be reconsidered, for example, as a mode of self-expression. Should we consider the positive and communicative side of the matter, and revise a metaphorical system that partly stiffens our way of seeing things?

Sometimes analysis becomes boring for patients, and they say that it is an old discipline, that it is a stale, musty science, that is smells like grandma's clothes, because we keep using a completely obsolete conceptual apparatus. It's like using 1902s scalpels in today's operating theatres, even though electrosurgical knives have been invented and today we have laser scalpels too. There are so many concepts that are part of our history, that it is important to have had, that have been valuable but that we no longer need.

Let's quickly retrace the history of psychoanalysis: after Freud we had Melanie Klein, who would deserve a Nobel Prize just for saying that internal reality is as real as external reality, for having the foolish courage, during the bombing of London, as V2 rockets were flying over the house she was working in, to keep interpreting Richard's drawings, viewing V2 s as attacks he wanted to direct at his mother's breast. Only a madwoman could say that the V2 flying above was an attack on the breast, just as the V2 was flying over her house, right?

There have been some revolutionary minds. Think of Winnicott or Bion. Then we have all the junk, that is, all that conceptual apparatus that we no longer need but that we keep hauling around. For this reason, analysis becomes a terrible bore. The analyst who does not answer your questions, the analyst who does not shake your hand, the analyst who does not wish you a happy Easter, the analyst who does nothing but interpret, the know-it-all analyst who makes you feel stupid, the analyst who interprets everything according to envy, or to some other concept he fixates on: psychoanalysis needs to be unburdened. The analyst should be someone who travels with just his hand baggage. You know one of those small trolley suitcases, the ones you're allowed to bring aboard a plane and can be stored in the overhead bin? There, that should be our luggage, instead of twelve suitcases with all the psychoanalytic paraphernalia from two centuries ago. Lightweight luggage, hand luggage, and just that. You know Western movies? What did the cowboy have? A horse, a lasso, and a Winchester. Sometimes a pan and some beans, that was all. A cowboy travelling with a full set of trunks would be unheard of.

> Several questions sprang to my mind at once. The first is, did psychoanalysis and psychoanalytic institutions definitively give up any attempt at maintaining cohesion, and also at mourning for the changes in theories. Physicians read the texts from the last decade, plus a few classics. Analysts trace the history from its beginning, and have to have read Freud, Ferenczi, Abraham, Anna Freud, Klein, Winnicott, Bion, Kohut, Green, Laplanche and Pontalis, Meltzer, Rosenfeld, Bollas, Heimann, Etchegoyen, Ogden, Kernberg, Aulaigner, Mitchell, Gabbard, McWilliams, the Barangers, and maybe Lacan, if they are brave. Even this meagre list betrays a certain basic ignorance of the psychoanalytic landscape. And I withhold the names of the Italians, who would be dozens. Only then can they try to chase down contemporary psychoanalysis, that is running fast in the meantime.
>
> It so happens that everybody builds their own personal theory, but don't we run the risk—which is perhaps an opportunity, I don't know—of feeling confused in the midst of all these theories, or of really struggling to build communication bridges? Because then we risk talking to each other a bit like autistic individuals, each one lost in his own world, experiencing difficulty in conversing, in linking concepts together. Each analyst has his own

transference on theories and authors, so that each concept has its share of admirers, and cannot be put aside. So, what can we do? Do we keep everything? Do we vote on which concepts to suppress?

We're like a family that has not emptied its closets for 200 years, that hoards as certain psychotic individuals do: hoards and hoards, so that we have concepts that are part of the history of psychoanalysis, but have outlived their usefulness. For this reason, a travelling analyst is followed by twenty-four carriages full of trunks, of junk that is no longer useful.

Let's make a few enemies: tell me three things we need to dispose of!

Freud's work.
    As far as its clinical use today is concerned, it is useless: reading something from Freud is never going to be helpful in a clinical situation. Things are different if you read Freud to see the method he used, he dared to change all the time. We do the greatest injustice to Freud when we say, "Freud said it all." No, he said brilliant things, but what he left us and what is still alive is his method, while I do not think that there is almost any concept, except general concepts such as the importance of the dream, of the unconscious, of sexuality, that endures as he had theorised it. Today many of us do not think of the unconscious as Freud theorised it, the sexuality Freud talked about is not the one we are discussing today. So I would not find any reason why we should read Freud's work, except for flavour, the pleasure of knowing history at the time of our grandparents, or to read a few clinical cases that are delightful, but certainly not to do the same to our patients. In the Wolf Man (1918b) there is that dream where there's a wolf outside the window, with its ears pricked up. The patient tells of how as a child he had had that dream, and then there is the encounter with the primal

scene, but today it is clear that what the patient is saying is different: "I feel oppressed by the idea that you're behind me with your ears pricked up, ready to tear me to pieces at any time!"

If we think about Freud's way to interpret dreams, looking for condensation, displacement, symbolisation, one wonders: who interprets a dream like that today? Today we interpret dreams differently.

> So, for example, suppose you were the president of the Psycho-analytic Society of San Marino and you had to work on a training system, would you recommend summarising Freud's work? I think of Quinodoz's *Reading Freud* (2004) and others.

I once jokingly proclaimed myself president of the Finnish Society, some forty people, less hot-headed than us, with an apparently less passionate disposition. I would have Freud's clinical cases read in the Finnish Society: they are entertaining because they are from another time. When Freud goes to visit that poor eighteen-year-old girl and he talks about her sexual feelings towards him, she has this dream with a great fire and interrupts her analysis: if in the early twentieth century a doctor went and told a girl of eighteen, "You desire me!", dreaming about the house burning down and her flight and stopping analysis was the least that she could do. But we should say this: those things are so obvious that why we cannot see them is a mystery. So, were I San Marino's president, I would have them read Jean Michel Quinodoz's excellent book, because we have to know the basics of where we started from, and cultivate a taste for history. Quinodoz performs an intelligent operation, he explains how from this or that Freudian concept developed these or these other conceptual lines. I would have them read, as I said, Freud's clinical cases, and that's it. I would devote to Freud ten per cent of the time: it seems enough. Then I would have them read Winnicott because he is alive and vital, the things he says are still very relevant, even in clinical practice; Klein should not be skipped for this revolutionary idea according to which the inner world is as important as the outer one. And then Bion, for his method. But he worked poorly: if you read "Attacks on Linking" (1959), you understand from its interpretations that he did not free himself from Klein. In his work method, that is, he was still Kleinian, he told the patient a lot of nonsense. Going from memory, he interprets the patient like this: the patient tells him that he sees someone's hand, he feels someone's hand stabbing him with a knife and he replies to the patient that he had a hallucination, instead of understanding that what he had said was a stab. But Bion is also the one who held the Seminars (1974, 2005a, 2005b; Aguayo & Malin, 2013), the one who gave us tools such as the alpha function and who offered us all those stimuli that allowed us to develop new theories and to go on into the unknown, as did Grotstein, who unsurprisingly titled one of his books *Do I Dare Disturb the Universe?* (1981). To say nothing of that troublemaker Ogden; I call him a troublemaker because he forces us to rethink, to restart our thought.

But I repeat that I would travel with a very lightweight luggage; in order to be a good analyst I think that one should have done a long and well-done analysis, well-done because there is no perfect analysis. One should have done a good analytic work, digging with a hoe, with a tractor; the tool used is not even very important, because in analysis a lot more things happen than those that we know about. Analytic research is naming these things. This is our future, finding out why it works, but we'll find out more the more we will be able to give up grandma's feather hat. Some things such as penis envy are absurd: speaking of which, there is that joke about two kids, you know it?

Please tell me.

There's this boy who walks up to a girl and shows her his pee-pee, feeling all proud, and tells her, "Look, I have this, and you don't!" And the girl calmly lowers her panties and replies: "Yes, but with this thing that I have, I can have as many I want!"

This joke should suffice to dismantle penis envy. What penis envy? Of course, in 1892 there might have been envy for the freedom enjoyed by men, and the intricacies that derived from that, but what's the point in thinking today in terms of penis envy?

> On the other hand there are many analysts who gladly do without what some say is a different psychotherapy, that is similar to psychoanalysis, but is not psychoanalysis. In some regions they work with a Freudian architecture and with its evolutions mostly of the French tradition, and thus they practise a different type of psychoanalysis than the one you suggest. At this point one wonders whether a deep consideration on clinical research would be expedient—be it done with the patients' help, with observations of analysts, through the judicious use of tests, or even with neuro-imaging—to see whether a given method, a given type of conceptual apparatus is useful or not in clinical practice, and how. I fear that in some of our scientific meetings we end up discussing like in those political debates. Everybody brings interesting ideas and experiences, complete with case studies as examples, but do we not sometimes risk an ideological drift? A fragmentation in self-referential and competing monads?

I do not think that "French" analysis is ineffective; I would say that analysis has such a transformative potential that the very act of doing it, even with the most antiquated tools, eventually gives results, because what really matters is basically how I feel listened to, how I feel understood, how much are my projective identifications accepted by the mind, how do you transform them and return them to me in the form of thought. What matters, that is, is what the two minds do together, which still largely happens unknowingly. Many analyses, indeed, work despite the analyst's clumsiness.

If we want to talk about politics and psychoanalysis, then I think we are still in the Middle Ages, we are still in an age of barons. There are many barons, each with his own land.

Or his own field.

Or his field. Each has his field, and woe betide anyone hunting deer in the land of the king, of the baron, because we all know how it ends.[3] And the same goes for models. There are even entire regions characterised by a certain approach: we know what kind of analysis to expect in Chicago, what kind of analysis to expect on average in Buenos Aires, and so on.

So in psychoanalysis there is a close connection between geography and the manifestation of power. The psychoanalysis of the SPP (Paris Psychoanalytical Society) is completely different from British psychoanalysis.

This is very true, and in my opinion the main difficulty of doing research is the lack of appropriate tools: I think we are still at the level of epidemiological research. We have not yet developed the tools, the ones we have now are quite shoddy. I think it would not hurt to find out more.

Then there is this big trouble, that is, that I still think that analysis—as much as I would love it to be considered by everybody a science—from a certain professional point on inevitably becomes an art. I believe that the same happens in other scientific fields. It is very likely that a senior vascular surgeon still belongs to the realm of science, but I believe that a vascular surgeon, at some point, might make a leap that truly makes him a unique artist of the scalpel. Even though his practice remains absolutely practical! At some point though I think in a molecular biologist, even in a surgeon, even in hard sciences, a process is triggered that borders on and encroaches on the artistic. I think this happens in analysis a few lucky times; when this happens, finding the quantitative tools to evaluate these artistic aspects becomes very complex, very hard: bless the day when we will possess, we will have invented new measuring tools!

Here, however we cannot think that in order to do research in psychoanalysis we have to observe how many times does the analyst use the word "separation" and if that analysis is more effective than one in which the word "separation" is not used. It is still a very rough level of research, so I wish for the time when we will be able to make some sensible research, able to capture some relevant nuclei regarding what is happening.

It is not easy, because it is not even easy to insert a person, a viewer, in the field of observation, not to mention the very stuff of our observation. Shall we do as Thomä and Kächele (1988) did, who had done research on recorded sessions? But a session, when recorded, is not the same as it would have been without a recorder, both on our part and the patient's.

I still think that the best way to convey a session is to narrate it later, or to write a protocol like when one pens the sessions, even though that is inevitably a lie relative to O. That is, considering the session as O—the thing itself—we can study his narrative derivatives. It is the same problem as supervision: if I have a recorded session, I will consider all of that material with the same unit of measure; instead a session that went through the "colander" effect of rewriting, that is, that has let the least significant things leak away and has kept the most important ones, is much easier to supervise.

So, I think that the central theme you are touching on is the relationship between past and future, or what space we have to leave for the unknown, and what we have to sacrifice: sort of like how the session is "drained", the crucial issue of psychoanalytic epistemology is how much to "drain" theory?

I have to add something, using a strong metaphor: I fear paralysis and fossilisation very much, and I was just now imagining the analyst as one of those shelled animal species; I picture him crawling around with a house representing Freud's work on his back, and by all means I do not like to imagine him carrying a heavy calcareous concretion on his shoulders. I'd prefer a different species, a species able to evolve by leaving aside the less useful parts.

And now, as ISIL is destroying Palmyra's monuments, there is a huge number of psychoanalysts across the world going "full astern", going back to the blissful 1910s, '20s, and '30s, because the future scares us I think; what's new scares us as a species, the alien scares us, everything that we do not know scares us, partly because it's our own alien elements, activated when confronted by what's new, that scare us.

I don't know, I'm a good guy, middle class, from a good family … so where are my alien elements?

Who wants to know them though? Why should I know them, what is the reason that would prod me deal with them?

If anybody comes to me and gives me some small comfort, reassures me, I can go back to being a librarian: dining with my wife every Saturday night, raising children who will in turn be librarians, so why should I go and touch this stuff?

After all, analysis should be this: getting in touch, not having cities with roads closed to traffic, not having cities with prohibitions on transit, being able to pass through every street in our current mind and indeed conceiving it as a constantly expanding mind.

So we need a little bit of ISIL. If we keep worshipping what we know, we become like UNESCO heritage sites ourselves. And here I want to remark how lucky Americans are at this time, because, despite what some claim, today psychoanalysis is more lively in the USA than where the waltz is danced—the waltz's charm notwithstanding.

I was recently in Stockbridge which is the last psychoanalytic centre of total therapy for serious patients in the world. I must say that they are absolutely unafraid of the new, to them the new is a category towards which there is really incredibly easy access and enthusiasm. I believe that the reason for this openness is because, when I was in Stockbridge, colleagues were proud of the hotel where I was staying, The Red Lion, which was built in 1770; it was as if it were a Mesopotamian relic!

So their mind, their geography is not completely cluttered by all the already known. It shows in their lifestyle too: to relocate to San Francisco or New York and to travel with a light luggage, most of them usually store their old furniture, so they only bring along a bicycle and their clothes and move without any difficulty, while their family furniture is left somewhere.

On the contrary I have the feeling that we Europeans show a great difficulty in moving inside our models or in doing acts of insubordination towards our barons, partly because the barons still have a "power of life or death" on theories and on people.

We talked about the barons, handing down their title from father to son. Our analytic "fathers" are our analysts and supervisors. How do you become an analyst without going back to feudalism?

First, I would say that in order to become an analyst you need a good analysis, a long analysis, a playful analysis: this seems absolutely essential to me. I think supervisions are useful to understand how the various models work: I would not want two consistent supervisors, whereas it would be interesting to have two supervisors with widely different models, who could explain to me the whys of a certain way to work or another. Then I would choose.

Maybe I'd even like to do six months of supervision here and there, going to taste different flavours: cherries, but also mango. Above all you need to taste exotic fruit: I remember, by the way, when some absolutely unknown fruit arrived in Italy, and then invaded the supermarkets. We have to learn to get curious about what's new.

Second, I would simplify, for example in an issue concerning the two years of supervision, as demanded by our Italian psychoanalytic training, where there is a question whether the patients being treated have to be the same throughout the two years or you may change them. We are burdened by complications: we say that supervised analysis has to be at least two years long with the same patient in order to see the analytic process unfolding. I can examine how each analyst or aspiring analyst works in that session, and maybe help him work better than how he is at that moment. For example, when a candidate sees me for a supervision, he almost never hears me talk about the concept of field: it is not a concept that I introduce in my supervision, except if later a passion for that model is sparked in him. Obviously, he will not hear me talk about the transference–countertransference axis either. Meaning that he will hear me talk about the living things that are happening in the analytic situation, where there's just him and the patient, to help him use the tools at its disposal, even without knowing it.

Notes

1. Lewis Carroll (1871), *Through the Looking-Glass, and What Alice Found There.*
2. "I would not try to integrate at all costs on a principle. Sometimes there are situations where you have to do as the lizard does, sacrifice the tail to save yourself. So integration is as important as sometimes splitting is. It could be that we have to lose some aspects of ourselves along the road in order to be able to evolve, like the lizard's tail" (aside by Antonino Ferro).

3. Translator's note: A reference to the traditional ballad *Geordie*,
   popularised in Italy by singer-songwriter Fabrizio De André.

> Ah my Geordie will be hanged in a golden chain
> This is not the chain of many
> Stole sixteen of the king's royal deer, and he sold them in
>   Bohenny.

CHAPTER FIVE

The road from Freud to Bion

Some time ago I formed the idea that many analysts, in their professional history, retrace the history of psychoanalysis. Ontogeny retracing phylogeny. They begin by acknowledging the patient's crucial need to understand: I have to understand the patient and help him do the same. So insight, "analysis with the Ego" as Bolognini (1991) would call it, and the role of historical reconstruction are fundamental. Later on, the scales begin to tilt towards other aspects: the patient's need to feel he's being understood, and thus the focus shifts to Winnicott's holding (1960), Bion's at-one-ment and negative capability (1970), and analysis with the Self (Bolognini, 1991). Of course things aren't always so clear-cut, and maybe what I'm recounting is just my personal journey, but I think it's important for new analysts to think about the therapeutic value of the quality of listening.

What if we skipped the first part and started from the last?

That would be great!

What if we arranged training so that Ogden, Bromberg, and Grotstein would be taught first, and then we'd turn back, doing some Freud during the fourth year? I mean, I would completely turn the perspective on its head, because you have to give an analyst his operational tools: if he has an appointment with a patient at half past seven, why should I tell him how they used to interpret dreams back in 1912? Isn't it more interesting to tell him how Ogden, or someone else, would interpret a dream today? So, let's see Ogden, Grotstein, Bromberg, everyone picks who they relate to, and then we work backwards.

> Some would object that, if you are unfamiliar with Freud, you cannot understand Ogden.

I know that there are colleagues who oppose changes being made in that direction, they feel mutilated. But it is not true. If you ask me if there is a Freudian concept that I use in my clinical practice, there will be a few that I unconsciously use, certainly I use the concept of setting, I use the idea that dreams are important, but not more so than other forms of communication, I don't know what else. The point is that I'm more interested in what I do not know than in what I know, so I'm more interested in going towards the unconscious; but really, who has ever actually seen the primal scene?

> So, since you don't want to talk about the primal scene, let's talk about how psychoanalysis works. We have to help the patient work through his conflicts, work through his losses, work though the transfer or whatever we want to call it; however, if I then have to describe what I mean by working through, things get complicated. Thinking for an instant, the first images that sprang to my mind were a cow in the middle of a meadow that ruminates grass to a pulp and then swallows it, or a dispersible aspirin tablet that has to be dissolved in water, which the analyst stirs with a spoon and acts as a "working through aid". They are surely nice and polished metaphors, but we can be more specific in describing the work that keeps us busy for months and for years on end—psychic working through—and that oftentimes is not described

in the books except with a generic "we worked it through for months". What does it mean to psychically work through?

I believe that, with experience, it takes about half an hour to get a general idea of the patient's issues, of what are his uninhabitable satellites or some of his unknown worlds. When a patient comes in and says: "My aunt is a nun … as a child she did not allow me to play with Barbie dolls … I joined the Girl Scouts …"[1] you know that there's a split can-can dancer; where did the can-can dancer go?

So the beginning of the analytical work, which can be time-consuming, will be to go and find the can-can dancer. It is a matter of opening some occluded, impassable worlds. And for the patient's defensive organisation, having to go to the Moulin Rouge will be like for a cow to be brought to the slaughterhouse, because the patient has to slaughter her old way of inhabiting the world. There's a long way to go before reconciling the child who has never played with Barbie dolls, whose aunt was a nun, who made promises to God when she was a little girl, with the idea of crossing the Moulin Rouge street, and then maybe hanging out there, and then possibly dancing the can-can there and thinking about flirting!

Then, walking, other worlds will open up of which we were at first utterly unaware: what's going to happen at the Moulin Rouge? We do not know, maybe the dancer will mess around with the knife thrower, then she'll leave him and hook up with the policeman, she'll be a prostitute or will join the Salvation Army; what really matters is that the patient is able to open up and inhabit ever new worlds. Already during the first interview we more or less understand what kind of movie we'll have to shoot early on in analysis, after that God only knows. But I think what really matters is being able to open up, to cross obstructed worlds.

Now I'm unsure whether to ask you about the maxim "without memory nor desire," (Bion, 1967) because it seems almost

> superfluous: perhaps this motto too has been used so much that it has become another feather on the hat. I'm going to ask you another, maybe cheekier question instead: can we give up free association?

We can give up free association the instant we accept that there is none, while there is obligated association, meaning that our mind is capable of no freedom except associating the most various and diverse narrative derivatives to waking dream thought that is being structured; that is, what we have always mistaken for free associations are obligated associations stemming from that film of waking dream thought that is taking shape in our minds without us knowing it.

> I'll rephrase the question: can we give up the method of free association? Or should we keep it for now?

I would give up any preconceived method. I repeat, I think that the method of free association has been replaced by the method of obligated dream, that is, given a situation, given a patient, given an analyst, then they have to make that specific dream, they are not free at all. I think that the waking dream thought is the key to this revolution, but we should not think that history ends with the French Revolution!

So this is a revolution, I hope with all my heart that within forty years there will be another revolution and that the concept of field will be forgotten, that no one will think about it anymore. Now, however, the great revolution, not yet rooted deeply enough in psychoanalytic thinking, is Bion's. Bion is treated like a nice feather in the hat; anyone who merely quotes him presumes to know Bion.

But the shocking concept that Bion reveals to us, as I have said time and again, is that there is a process that continuously transforms the data that we receive from reality, so that reality is continuously being transformed into a movie sequence within our mind. This process comes to life in a still largely unknown way, but it happens and happens in every mind, and this is the specificity of our species. We do not know whether other species do it, but I would say that our species is the one that does it the most; that is, we continuously transform the sensory flow, the flow of stimuli into a sequence of pictograms, into a dream sequence unknown to us. Our whole mental life depends on this dream sequence of pictograms that we do not know: we hang from this sequence of pictograms like our ancestors hung from tree branches, assuming they did. We cannot break away from that, so there is no method of free association, there is instead a method that acknowledges the importance of dreams and of this sequence of pictograms that is continuously being formed in our mind and from which all possible stories then originate. It is with this narrative construction that we can have fun; we are free to use any possible narration, which has to be consistent with the dream sequence in continuous production with our mind, thus our degree of freedom is very relative.

> Now, however, please keep in mind that to the patient I'm going to see after the holidays, with whom I agreed to do two sessions a week—because three felt too risqué to him—I have to set the fundamental rule, which is to think aloud, trying not to select his thoughts, so we are in free association territory.

Why?

> Give me an alternative then, because I have to see that patient!

I would greet the patient with a smile, rather the first time I would tell him, look, I wanted to tell you that when we start the analysis, if you feel like it you can lie on the couch, which sometimes allows one to feel freer and to work better. I would not give any indication to the patient, I would not tell him what to do or not to do, because basically doing that is to renounce Satan! And why should I renounce Satan? Why do I have to tell you what passes through my mind? That fundamental rule is already setting analysis on railroad tracks. However, if the patient wants to play with the coins that he carried in his pocket, are we supposed to forbid him? No, when the patient arrives, we give him a space of free expression, which is not free because it depends on the dream sequence he set. So when the patient arrives I would tell him, "Please, make yourself at home, if you feel like it you can lie on the couch." And I wait. If he does not speak, after three, four, or five minutes I would ask something like, "Why this silence?"

Because I don't know what to do!

Well, let's make it up! Maybe we can start with "Tell me something!" I think that giving a pre-made indication, "You have to tell me what comes to your mind!" is already a very strong closing, it's apparently freedom, but it is no opening; that is, you tell him right away: "Look, you can't do anything else, huh! What are you thinking! Do not even think about doing something else!"

Exactly!

And if one wants to sob, wants to laugh, wants to masturbate, wants to play with the toy soldiers he brought with him, why are we supposed to inhibit his freedom of expression? "Relative" freedom of expression, at least in a social sense. Because outside the social sense he is obligated to go in the direction that his waking dream thought drives him to, because we cannot escape our waking dream thought. We continuously shoot a movie about ourselves and about what is happening to us. We close this movie and we no longer hear about it, because it lies beyond the *contact-barrier*. This movie is then told to us through narrative derivatives, that in progressive steps towards consciousness change the meaning of the original pictograms, like in a children's "game of telephone" or "Chinese whispers."

So, if for example we have a persecutory anxiety state (a "someone dangerous and threatening" pictogram), maybe he will tell it like a thriller: there is a dangerous man chasing me with a knife. Or he tells it like an everyday event: "Last night I saw on television an Israeli submarine chasing ..." or he tells it like any other genre, it does not matter. But the thing that we analysts have not yet understood is the obligatory nature of the waking dream thought. The dream is no longer central, but according to Bion's theory as we understand it today, what really matters is how the alpha function forms the first Lego bricks, that is, how there is a printing machine that prints green, red, blue Lego bricks and creates a mandatory sequence, after which it says: "What do we do now? Let's play, guys!" From that moment on, you can play as you want!

All games are possible and allowed, but there is something crucial: in order to play, to this date, we needed those Lego bricks. Our mind cannot play in another way: for now the only game that our mind can play is one with Lego bricks.

So there is an obligatory nature, that is the sequence of bricks that the machine continuously gives you, transforming reality's stimuli.

See that book with a yellow spine over there on the book-shelf? Maybe now the alpha absorbs the yellow and creates a yellow Lego brick, then there is a blue one there, it absorbs the blue and makes a Lego brick of the same colour. Sequences derive from this absorption from reality. As soon as you get to a given quantity, they fall down and can be used. So, at some point, anyone finds himself having a large amount of Lego bricks, and then he is ready to play by inventing what he wants, limited to what the mysterious printing machine offers as raw material. This is Bion's greatest discovery, which I think is psychoanalysis' most important after the discovery of the unconscious. So the alpha function is forever building Lego bricks, and until there should be an evolutionary leap for the species, this machine will keep doing the same job. When there will be an evolutionary leap of the species, we do not know what will happen next! For now, and I think for the next one hundred thousand years, our species will keep producing Lego bricks that derive from the yellow book, the green bauble, and so on. Then we find ourselves having all those baskets filled with bricks to play with as we want, but it is still a relative freedom, because it depends on the types of bricks that have been produced.

This way of seeing things completely revolutionises psychoanalytic thought, something that analysts should be happy with, whereas most do not want to hear about it.

But if I do not like Bion, I just do not like him and that's it; if I like Winnicott instead, why should the future of psychoanalysis depend on those bricks, without free association?

You can practise psychoanalysis as you want! There has to be freedom, freedom of the model and freedom to throw away all of Bion's works, why not? Maximum freedom to everybody.

The difference between the two is that Winnicott didn't theorise a model of the mind, Winnicott was a great clinician. Bion was in my opinion a very poor clinician instead, at least before the turning point of *Learning from Experience* (1962): he worked in a way that I find unconvincing, because he did not free himself from Klein; poor thing, it was none of his fault. But he was a great theorist: Bion gives us a completely new and shocking metapsychology, that many do not know, but it's a metapsychology that opens new doors and windows.

Bion's model makes us take a true leap in knowledge, going from the horse to the horsepower. From this new metapsychology derives a completely different technique, so if someone does not know Bion's model then he cannot access the new technique that follows from it. He was a genius; it is not our fault that after Freud we had another genius. Can we ignore him? Sure.

Now I suggest to you a less provocative and perhaps more sensible consideration. I understand that besides all the technical adjustments and theoretical backgrounds, we are faced with two widely different metapsychological architectures. From a structural sense of belonging to one or the other, be it the result of a choice—as we know—more or less unconscious, also derives the way to practise one's own psychoanalysis. At this juncture, how is it possible for those who adopt a Freudian metapsychology, and thus move from a series of assumptions such as frustration as the driving force of desire, to accept the downgrading of abstinence, of silence as the driving force of transference, and so on?

I find this thing very funny, and I hope the hilarity that these concepts cause in me does not offend anyone, that is, still thinking that frustration provides desire, desire then lights the fuse, and so on …

It amuses me that I have been an analyst for forty years and basically such a thought never remotely crossed my mind. I never knew it, it never interested me, and I do not think I was a lousy analyst after all.

These concepts never affected me. I have been affected by other things, so I would say this: there is an entirely different model of the mind. There is a metapsychology derived from Bion that is completely different from the one derived from Freud, and the two will never be comparable. What are the similarities and differences between the ego and the alpha function?

Eh …

None! It's not like comparing two languages related to Latin: "I" in French becomes "Je", in Italian we say "Io".

No. Bion's model, *if* we really accept it, is incompatible with any other model. But then nobody really accepts it, now that's the tragedy: indeed Bion's model has been seriously considered, with the resulting changes, by very few people. I could mention Grotstein, I could mention Ogden, and there are many others; I could mention Corrao, closer to us. Others mostly use Bion as a feather in their hat. Instead Bion's model is a strong model, incompatible with others.

If we start from the fundamental aspect, this Lego-printing machine, then we have an entirely different metapsychology, from which follow the pathology of the printer, the pathology stemming from a lack of plastic to make Lego bricks, or maybe we have too many bricks. Consequently the theory of technique is revolutionised too.

Everybody agrees on Winnicott for a reason: he was an excellent clinician. He does not have a particularly strong theory, because it is a bit Freudian, a bit Kleinian, a bit Winnicottian. Jokingly, we might say that Winnicott is almost like the Red Cross. A nice person, a paediatrician, everybody loves him, because he is the uncle that we all wish we had.

No, not Bion. Bion implies a strong choice, including the choice to say that clinically Bion was not worth much compared to what he theorised, in the sense that he was a strictly orthodox Kleinian when he worked: this he had been taught, and this he did.

But then he was a genius in theoretical work and in clinical seminars, where he began to make his theory work in the way of doing supervision. There's that beautiful passage—I do not remember it exactly—in which he notes that it would be amazing to be able to look through the pharynx until you can see the bottom and vice versa. Bion was Picasso, he is comparable to Picasso when he breaks the figure, because he depicts a face as seen from the right, from the left, from the front at the same time and put it all on the canvas. Picasso does a quantum leap in figurative art, just like Bion. Then one is allowed to say: "I do not like it." Where's the problem?

What does not work is if someone who works in this way appears before an examination board and he's asked *where* is the frustration of desire ... One doesn't even try answering that question, it is obvious that they speak two different languages.

At this juncture the problem is how to …

… accept that there are at least two metapsychologies.

Indeed. And if you have to structure a model of training, it is necessary to account for this plurality which can be hardly integrated: either you ignore it, or you split things up like in postwar Berlin.

Or you split things up, as the British Society did to resolve disputes between Anna Freud and Melanie Klein. Say what you will about the British, they are so serious. When they perceived that there was no room for agreement, they organised three analytical formations: a classical one, a Kleinian one, and an intermediate one for an independent group. Now they are fewer in number, so they got back together.

We pretend that clinical thought erodes any theoretical distance, and those who come to the institution do so by toning down conflicts, especially if they are in the minority like those who have a viewpoint inspired by Bion or by field theory. So maybe they present themselves in a much more classic style, emphasising the transference/countertransference axis, bringing a couple of dreams, an interpretation or three and the rest is easy. And then they add something sexual, just to keep the attention level up. Then we might ask what does sexuality have to do with analysis, but that would be another can of worms.

What do we say to that poor 70 per cent or 80 per cent of readers mainly trained on Freudian metapsychology that got up to this point, in Chapter 5, and are wondering, more or less: "If an integration, that is not rudimentary like a feather in the hat, is really difficult, do I have to begin exploring Bion at my ripe old age of forty, fifty, or sixty to then re-found my way to work?"

I think we should start thinking like that silly song by Jo Squillo suggested, that went like: "We are women, there's more besides the legs!". I would say: "There's more besides Freud." You can go beyond the first thing that strikes you.

> The problem though is the depth of change in internal structure required, not just to read a book by Antonino Ferro, but to acquire a theory that seems to collide with one's own starting model.

Exactly. I repeat that it cannot be integrated, they are just two different things.

> Take it or leave it.

Take it or leave it. I'm interested in it, I'm not interested in it. I just wish it was not ostracised. The fact that I was allowed to be the SPI's president maybe means that it is not automatically banned. Maybe, I'm not sure.

Then there are bright people that I admire, that I love, who are trying to integrate the models; I just can't do it. In Italy Anna Ferruta is trying to do that, Giuseppe Civitarese endured a lot in trying to reconcile Freud with Bion, working on transformations in hallucinosis in Freud and Bion (Civitarese, 2015). Now he is completely "fielded", I think he'll be the one to carry forward this principle, unless he opens other avenues.

Then there's the fact that I'd be glad to know that the concept of field will extinguish itself, and that then there will be a concept, in continuity or discontinuity with it, that allows us to work ever better and to make people suffer as little as possible.

> Isn't it in some ways more convenient to strongly criticise Freudian "liturgy" from a Bionian position, which is obviously much wider, while firmly clinging onto one's own Bionian metapsychological structures?

Keep in mind however that there is now a post-Bion: we have an evolving post-Bionian metapsychology and, perhaps, there was a jump, and it is the fourth jump since the Barangers' original field theory (1961–1962), that of cross-fertilisation of Bion's thought with the concept of field, which is another thing, that is no longer the concept of field created in a completely different way, outside Bion. From the moment we combine post-Bion with fourth-generation field, it is no longer a Bion that talks about analysis in the terms that Bion used. The field model, when it is coupled with Bion, becomes a powerfully growing field. Then it is not a given that in that field you have to grow beets and only beets. After the beets there will be the year of cherries, then another year still, and then we'll see what will happen, although I fear that for now the majority prefer *ortodossia*[2] to the field.

> Let's play a game: I'll read you a short comment that an agoraphobic patient of mine made yesterday, but let's pretend that it was told by Psychoanalysis itself.
>
> "The paradox is that over time I got to the point of avoiding the things that I like the most: I've always loved being with people, doing stupid risky stuff, travelling to some faraway place for a concert, going on holiday with a lot of friends. It is really absurd that I gave it all up on purpose. This gave me a strong desire to change things a little bit. Even in small things, exchanging words with someone I don't know or I'm just getting acquainted with at the coffee machine satisfies me more than being able to do something difficult at work; however, I always involuntarily manage to meet new people, even though in practice I always go to the same places. I never go to new places. It's as if my subconscious outwitted me and showed me new people to meet, even though I avoid the places where you usually meet new people."
>
> Does psychoanalysis suffer from agoraphobia?

Well, I would say that perhaps reading this little story to candidates during the first year would be much more useful than telling them to never use other metaphors than those the patient himself provided, more useful than insisting on "flattening" them by putting all the already known on their shoulders. I think it would open new avenues to the candidates: I find this description simply beautiful, especially if it is put in the mouth of Psychoanalysis asking for a different treatment.

One thing that I do not like, and maybe it is time to say it, is when we're talking about the transference/countertransference axis. The transference/countertransference axis reminds me so much of the Rome-Berlin Axis, and we all remember well what disasters caused the Rome-Berlin Axis; I'd like not to hear about the transference/countertransference axis anymore.

Firstly because, as Bion says, we could only know our countertransference if we went to an analyst to let him analyse it, so we have absolutely no idea what our countertransference is.

And then, I think that the existence of this "mirror" axis makes sense if it is connected to a model, although I think it is an outdated model. I think it is something like the anti-typhoid serum: with all due respect to the anti-typhoid serum, which saved many people in the past, if someone gets sick with typhoid today we just give him some antibiotic, and in a few days he is well. I mean that certain concepts were useful while we were still, for example, within a relational theory, where many still stand.

The concept of field, whether we like it or not—we may well not like it and we may well ignore it—has no room for outdated formulations, for old axioms, such as the axis: there is neither transference nor countertransference anymore. There is a multi-group situation, constantly moving like sea waves and in perennial constant transformation, so we have to leave behind the transference/countertransference axis.

More generally speaking, the thing that irritates me is the a-historicity of psychoanalysis, shared by many colleagues; it means considering that what was true continues to be true, as if there was some kind of peculiarity of analysis and analysts that leads us to be like Amish people, who refuse to use the car or the phone: we keep using the horse, the cab, the black hat, and so on. It is as if it was unacceptable that, as in microbiology or any other branch of medicine, science, or art, there were evolution and change; of course *where id was, there ego shall be*: we got that, now let's move on.

As soon as we understand something, that thing should no longer interest us: we should be interested in the next one that we have not yet understood. Fixating on those few things that we understood as if they were the truth is the most *anti*-thing that could ever exist, but not in the sense of antimatter, which is something wonderful that we know, but *anti-* in the sense of anti-knowledge, anti-future, anti-charm of discovery. We already talked about the light pollution of Oedipus, which prevents us from seeing millions of other things that cross the field. It's time to obscure Oedipus to allow all other configurations, all other emotional and affective constellations, that are undergoing a revolutionary change, to be appreciated, because there are many more. We should not fixate on Orion and only look at that star; at some point we know what Orion looks like. But there are millions of other constellations. The constellations in our starry canopy seem like dozens, sure, but if we look at the universe we can find millions of constellations.

So beyond the already known there lies the charm of psychoanalysis, the fascination of science, our infinite abyss of ignorance, the infinite abyss of things we do not know and in which we should dive, enjoying it wildly; instead we entrench ourselves in those few things that we already know, cursing and putting at the stake those who dare to say something new.

This is something that makes me angry.

Notes

1. Translator's note: Most of the Italian Scouting movement is denominational and affiliated to Catholic organisations. "Being a Scout" carries implications of having had a religious upbringing.
2. Translator's note: Untranslatable play on the words *orto* (It. orchard) and *ortodossia* (It. orthodoxy).

CHAPTER SIX

Travelling light

S o, since we have to travel a long way, and most importantly with a light luggage, let's at least try to choose it carefully. In our articles there are a few successful concepts that, by dint of being used a lot, end up being used all the time. Sometimes they become master keys that can open any door. The concept of reverie, so poetic and evocative, lends itself to this fate. "And then I had a reverie!", as if it was an epiphany. What is it exactly?

I would start from what Grotstein says when he explains that the concept comes from Bion, but then spread like wildfire across all conceptualisations of psychoanalysis, so it is one of those umbrella concepts that after a while could mean everything and its opposite, sort of like the term "projective identification", so we can't understand each other. I would favour an extremely restrictive use of the concept. Let's first try to describe it clinically, then let's see its theoretical origin. Clinically I think it is when in the mind of an analyst, in the consulting room— we're retreading what we said about the analyst only existing when he also has a patient in a setting—an image presents itself insistently and annoyingly. These are the two important features: insistent and grating. It is something that at first disturbs the analyst: he wonders why it crosses his mind, he tries to get rid of it because it's annoying, because it interferes with that state of mind in which one is ready to listen, with a receptive state, it is something that really imposes itself on the analyst. And this image that imposes itself is usually something that has to do with the analytic situation in which one finds himself. Let's take a very simple example, which I have already discussed elsewhere: while I was with a patient, at some point the image of a sailing ship, one of those miniature ones inside a bottle, started coming to my mind—or to impose itself, I would say. I tried driving this image out because it was disturbing until, after the second and then the third time it returned to my mind, I resigned myself: "Oh well, I cannot drive it away, this image, surely it must mean something." Here, only when I accepted this, was I able to reflect on it; it seemed clear to me that this image was a picture of a situation experienced within the analysis and that it basically depicted a situation of *impasse*. In a situation where there is a sailing ship inside a bottle you do not travel. It represented one of those situations pictured by Conrad,[1] when he described the situation in which the ship finds itself when there is no wind, motionless in a state of dead calm, without going anywhere. Reflecting on that image, something that I did not previously know became clear to me, that is, that I had not realised we actually were in a stalemate in the analytic situation, we were in a situation of impasse. This is very different from the metaphor, in the sense that the metaphor is when I use an image of something of which I am aware, the better to share it with the patient. For example, if I have realised that in this analysis we are in a situation of impasse, I can use a metaphor: "It seems to me that our situation resembles that described by Conrad, when the ship is adrift and there is no wind," so I use a metaphor to share and spin into a narrative a metaphorical image of which I am already aware.

The linchpin of reverie is that it brings me something of which I have no knowledge. This is the most significant difference.

But reverie is not a one-size-fits-all concept. Behind it there's a specific theoretical model, which is to say Bion's, according to which we have a daytime dream activity during which the so-called alpha function, that is, the matrix of the diurnal dream, continuously produces images. Such images build the waking dream thought, which in turn will build the Lego bricks of our thought and of our dream as well, and reverie is the phenomenon by which I can get in touch with one of these bricks that were shaped by the alpha function from the senses and that the mind of each of us keeps building. So it is only reverie in the strict sense when, during a session, while I'm building without knowing a sequence of pictograms—sequences of aggregates of alpha elements—at one point one of these pictograms, instead of remaining hidden from myself, becomes something with which I come into contact. So I behold the opening of a window on my psychic life, which gives me a key to understanding what's happening at that moment inside the story that I'm living with the patient. So it's like being able to open a window where the dream thought is taking shape, and through this opening seeing a frame of the movie that is being formed. So, I can deduce a set of useful information regarding what is happening. This aspect is closely related to Bion's thought, to the concept of waking dream thought. Then, since it is a concept that refers to many other aspects of psychoanalysis, it has been understood in a very broad sense, as everything that comes to mind at any time, everything becomes reverie, everything becomes a dream-like state. It has nothing to do with that, reverie is something very specific.

You mentioned projective identification, which is another one of current psychoanalysis' big question marks. Personally, I think I had to read about it at least ten times before I got a partial hold on it, whereas there are colleagues of mine—I envy them more than a bit—who can talk about it with great ease. In extreme cases, the patient almost appears to be able to manipulate the analyst like a puppet: "The patient made me feel anger, then boredom, then he benumbed me and then I fell asleep."

In the training programme, projective identification was considered like the powerful and primitive defence mechanism described by Melanie Klein. Then Bion and the following generations identified its communicative functions; today in some texts, like those about the analytical field, it seems to be considered almost like a continuous function of relationship between people. Is it so?

Even projective identification is a very broad concept, an "umbrella concept" that eventually groups everything. I would limit it a bit. At first there was a very strong idea of projective identification: at 2:15 pm there was projective identification. Then there was projective counter-identification, how the person who received projective identification experienced it, how he worked it through, and so on. Today I would see it in a different way: I would see it more with the idea that there is a continuous exchange of micro-evacuations from one mind to another, both from the patient towards the analyst and from the analyst towards the patient. We need a bit of *slang* here: beta elements—the senses—continuously travel from one mind to the other, and we can call this travel projective identification, which gets stronger the more beta elements, like aeroplanes, find an aircraft carrier on which to land. If they find an aircraft carrier it means that there is a receptivity by the analyst on which they can land, so there they will also find a situation in which they can be metabolised and digested, so there could be a reverie, as a result of projective identification. We already discussed reverie; it operates mostly along the visual axis, we almost all operate along the visual axis. Keep in mind that everything that concerns the dream workings—the formation of alpha elements, thus of images that syncretise the actual emotional state at that time—actually works according to all the organs of sense. We should talk not just of pictograms— thus visual images—but also of audiograms, olfactograms, kinesthesigrams, that is, we should take into account that we are dealing with all the senses. There are people, like musicians, who often operate more along the auditory register than along the visual; however, I'm talking about the visual register because I would say that 99 per cent of us human beings operate along the visual register. However, it should be remembered that every time, for completeness, we should be speaking of pictogram, olfactogram, audiogram, and so on.

> Before moving on to the next question I'll try to enact an "airlift" operation to save Freud, who's vanishing from this discussion. Just to gauge the level of processing on which we are, could we say that the alpha elements have something to do with the thing-presentations Freud talked about?

This is a vexed question. I don't really like making comparisons between different models; there are colleagues who really love pointing out continuities, I prefer to point out the discontinuities. The Freudian model has its own entirety, its own roundedness. I do not find it very useful to ask, for example, how does the ego differ from the alpha function. Sure, your question could be a legitimate question: the thing-presentation has something to do with pictograms? I really like to consider each model as if it was a work on its own. It's like asking what are the connections between Degas and Picasso, the painter I love the most. I just don't wonder that. I prefer to pursue Picasso's world and Degas's world, without venturing into the stylistic similarities between Picasso's blue period and the paintings of Degas; that does not interest me at all.

> Let me play on your love for Picasso: in Barcelona, where there is a museum dedicated to him, in the first rooms I saw that the young Picasso was an excellent classic portrait painter, a great academic painter. So he chooses to set aside those lines, that he knows so well, to devote himself to a new style, and so he gives a visual example for Ogden's words about forgetting psychoanalysis to

go discover the unknown with each patient. So, could we say that the operation of forgetting "academy" psychoanalysis can only be done after acquiring it? That having acquired a classic model is necessary to then leave it and go further? Or not?

I'm afraid that a bit of West Point[2] is necessary. And then you can go from there and tread other paths and other roads. Here, I do not think that West Point needs to be the Freudian model. I had a training in which West Point was very strongly Kleinian. We usually equate metapsychology with Freudian metapsychology: says who? Metapsychology may be Freudian, Kleinian, Bionian, and so on.

I think that maybe a starting membership is required precisely in order to be able to detach from it, so I like that in the first rooms of Picasso there are some quite classic paintings. Of course, though, Picasso then evolved, like Bion. There is a Bion who, in the early parts of his writings, is 98 per cent Kleinian. Then he goes on to free himself, he somehow betrays Klein's lesson, innovating in an absolutely catastrophic way. But in his way of working, Bion remains Kleinian with his patients to the end. Whereas he makes his real breakthrough as a theorist, introducing us to absolutely new and previously unthinkable tools such as the alpha function, the waking dream thought, the waking dream. He then makes an even more incredible breakthrough in his supervision seminars in Sao Paulo, New York, Los Angeles, where we can really see a genius at work, someone who has completely overturned the previous way of thinking, so much so that some very orthodox Kleinians say that after 1962 Bion went mad. He went mad because since '62 he is no longer Kleinian, but blazes a completely new trail.

I'd like to find a training institute, where they taught a strong Bionian metapsychology, but where twenty years later that is betrayed, outdated, and abandoned. What really matters is the concept of step: we made some steps that brought us where we are, but we have to build more steps that hopefully will bring us somewhere else again. The concept of orthodoxy instead is the opposite of that, it is the one in which we all identify with the already known. For example, there is no French work that does not feature the difference between sexes and the difference between generations. The fact that there are very few works, anywhere except in the United States, without a dozen references to Freud in the first five pages, I find is absolutely representative of this orthodox entrenchment.

> So let's get to Bion's metapsychology. While words such as interpretation, insight, working through belong to the analytical language since forever, the term transformation, dear to Bion, enters the analytical debate much later. I searched the archives of the main international journals, and before the Sixties the term did not exist, except as transformations in a broad sense. In Italy it was being talked about in the Eighties and Nineties. What is, in your opinion, the role of transformation in contemporary psychoanalysis and its relationship with interpretation?

I would say that interpretation was always a deciphering of sorts, that is, the patient said something and the analyst interpreted: "You think you told me this thing, but you actually told me this other thing." So he deciphered, he gave a deciphering key, from utterly ridiculous readings to less ridiculous ones, depending on the case. I think of extreme cases of supervision in which the patient said that he liked dunking his cookies in milk in the morning, and it just had to mean that he wanted to have sex with his girlfriend. There is a strong discontinuity with Bion because the concept of transformation is inherent in his thought. In classic thought interpretation was hugely important, and interpretation has something to do with insight: you're telling me this thing, but actually you're telling me another thing; I make you aware of this hidden message that is unconscious. Bion's thought is imbued with the concept of transformation instead, not just in the situations of the session though, but before that in the fact that the therapeutic act is the transformation of beta elements, that is of senses, of clouds of senses, of fragments of proto-mental, in alpha elements, that is, towards the image. The analytic work basically becomes the transformation of these proto-emotional, proto-significant, "proto-everything" states, in images, then in narremes, in unions of narremes, that is in narratives, and through these processes one contributes to the construction of thought, to the construction of emotion, and basically also to the construction of the unconscious. With Bion, the transformative element is what matters in the session too. The patient comes to the session with a stomach ache that then, at the end of the session, if things work out, will not be decoded—"You have a stomach ache for this reason," so there are a discovery and insight—but the stomach ache will subside, and instead of the stomach ache you have images, constructions, tales, stories. So, instead of having a stomach ache, you end the session saying that you'd kill, or that you had a dream where you killed, someone who was pestering you. There is no reason to say that the analyst, or the father or the mother enters the scene, instead you build a movie about someone who wants to kill someone else, and then we'll see.

> Proto-emotions, beta elements: don't they run the risk of becoming, in clinical practice, somewhat vague concepts, a hodgepodge of anything bad that's going on in a person's head (or in a corner of the field)?

Well, I think that the wording of beta elements, alpha elements, destructiveness maybe is a way by which we distance ourselves a bit and try to make a bit more scientific something that belongs to us, something rotten inside us. So, I think that in every human being, for various reasons, often for defensive reasons, often for reasons related to suffering, there are some strongly rotten aspects, that analysis however has to deal with. Because these workings, or these not-workings, these rotten agglomerations are what we have to deal the most with. We have to be able to dream them and, by dreaming them, to transform them.

> I really love the Freudian motto—brilliant in its polysemic ambiguity, sometimes overlooked in its Italian translation—"Wo Es war, soll Ich werden." Where id was, where there was "it", there I, ego, shall be: "I" both as identity, myself, and as psychical self-conscious ego. In other words I need to know more about myself, my desires, and my conflicts: what is at stake is a conscious knowledge, a self-representation. I wonder and I ask you if in this game of transformation that he was describing, the development of transformative capacity is related to the conscious knowledge of oneself or if the development of the alpha function is something that, paradoxically, could lead a patient to feel better without consciously discovering any more about himself.

Were I to take things to an extreme, I would say that analysis can lead a patient to develop his own tools for thinking, to learn to use them in order to feel better any time he suffers a bombardment of proto-emotional states, in other words, I would say that the patient becomes able to continuously transform proto-emotional and proto-sensory states into something more understandable. Maybe this happens partly as a logical consequence of greater self-awareness, but only partly so. I think that insight loses much of its central importance, precisely in favour of the transformation that we facilitate and of the acquisition not of knowledge about us, but instead of tools that allow us to mentally function in a better way. It is not a given that this will happen with every psychoanalysis inspired by Bion, or by someone else, but it happens with every analysis that works, because even without knowing it analyst and patient work through, metabolise, and transform beta elements in images. That is, in analysis there is a continuous transformation, even in an analysis that is considered Kohutian or

Freudian; it is not the historical reconstruction that starts the process, it is the method instead that at some point supports these transformations. Indeed, I think that research in psychoanalysis is essentially naming events that have been happening in the consulting room since the beginning of psychoanalysis. Projective identifications did not begin with Klein, and the same thing is true for reverie: those processes are there since the very first moment that two individuals were in a room in a therapeutic stance. Psychoanalytic research is finding out what those two people above are doing in a room besides talking.

> Two people in a room are in a relationship, and the centrality of this issue is recognised both by relational psychoanalysis and by Kleinian and Bionian approaches. In your opinion, what are the major differences and similarities between these models of working?

Regarding technique, I think there are differences, marked differences. The Kleinian model calls for a much more active, interpretive approach. In fact it expects interpretations of bodily fantasies and a constant interpretation of transference. The first Bionian model embraced the centrality of the interpretations of transference too. The concept that both shared was that there are two protagonists on the analytic scene. In all of these models, I think that the common denominator is the centrality of the analytic relationship, even though in Kleinian and Bionian models that relationship is evaluated from the point of view of internal phantasies. Nevertheless, the presence of more than one mind is an essential fact, and everything that happens is seen as the result of the exchange between two minds.

In his later work, Bion moves away from the concept of analytic neutrality, and from then on the starting point of any transformation implies the interaction of two minds at work.

I'm more familiar with the Kleinian and Bionian way of working than with the relational one, but I think that there are several shared points. The most significant aspect in analysis is not what happened in the past or during childhood, but the relationship between patient and analyst in the "here and now" of the analytic session, and it is exactly in the "here and now" that transformations take place.

Notes

1. "The Nellie, a cruising yawl, swung to her anchor without a flutter of the sails, and was at rest. The flood had made, the wind was nearly calm, and being bound down the river, the only thing for it was to come to and wait the turn of the tide.

    "The sea-reach of the Thames stretched before us like the beginning of an interminable waterway. In the offing the sea and the sky were welded together without a joint, and in the luminous space the tanned sails of the barges drifting up with the tide seemed to stand still in red clusters of canvas sharply peaked, with gleams of varnished spirits."

    —Joseph Conrad, Heart of Darkness.

2. West Point, in the State of New York, is the seat of the United States Military Academy. In war movies it became famous as the training site par excellence.

CHAPTER SEVEN

The analytic field

One of the most controversial issues in contemporary psychoanalysis is plurality of languages and of psychoanalytic models. Our readers will be geographically and theoretically rather heterogeneous too. Before talking about the model that you are personally working on, would you tell us what you think about the plurality of voices in psychoanalysis?

I think it would not make sense to have a single model in psychoanalysis: we have many, we all know what they are, and I think it is an asset for everybody that each has his own with which to debate with others. I think that this debate is a great asset. In this regard I think I found a fairly simple key to quickly identify which internal model our interlocutor has, and that is to observe how the characters that this analyst speaks about are considered. Characters might be seen as actual people, real, living, in the flesh, and here we are in a more traditional model; they might be considered as internal characters, inhabitants of the internal world of the patient, and here we are in a typically more relational or Kleinian model; they might be understood as affective holograms, as functions of two minds, as those actors who allow us to share a dream within the session, and here we are in the wake of the field model in its various theoretical formulations.

> New analysts might be interested in knowing, within the plurality of models we are talking about, how did an experienced analyst find his own voice, starting from the training period, and then during his professional maturation. What are the roots of Ferro's analytic field?

I was lucky enough to have an analyst and supervisors who followed different models. Having different models, it was always hard for me to try to understand why, given a specific communication, one interpreted in a certain way, another interpreted in another way, and only then did I experience the fact that there were different models and that each had its reference points, explicit and implicit. It then became crucial for me to try to learn and understand the various models, and so starting from one model—that I did not know was Bionian—I met a radically different Kleinian model, and so I then met the Winnicottian model, so I went through the Freudian model until I found what was my own model, which might be perhaps described as emerging from the encounter between many of Bion's theories and the way I and other colleagues later advanced the concept of field.

During my training I encountered the concept of the field but very tangentially, and only later did I join this model to Bion's theories. I remember saying at the conference on Bion in Boston, from which I remember a great work by Jim Grotstein (2009), that as a result of that conference I formally announced the engagement between Bion's theory and the field. Since then these two concepts have been growing for many years, coupling between themselves and generating what I think are interesting perspectives. Of course the other important aspect for my model was approaching narratology, which lent itself very well as a source of inspiration, even though narratology as a field is external to psychoanalysis. However, it made it possible to understand better and to make more well-rounded the concept of character, which has a long history in narratology, from more traditional versions where character equates person, then of character as the driving force of the story, and finally as character which is co-constructed by the reader and the author of the text.

Before the engagement with Bion, the concept of field grew in Argentina, at the Barangers'. How did it get there?

The field is given space in the thought of Merleau-Ponty (1945), but its origins are older still. The Barangers were the first to apply this concept to psychoanalysis. What intrigued me about their work was how they drew attention to the formation of blind spots in the session, that the Barangers called "bastions". These are areas of resistance formed by crossed projective identifications: the patient, that is, is not the only one responsible for their formation, but there is an unconscious collusion of sorts with the analyst. These blind spots require special attention by the analyst in order to be dissolved.

I found it crucial that the ramparts were created by the analytic couple.

Since then, the concept of the field continued to evolve independently, and in Italy it was used by Francesco Corrao (1986), who considered it as the sum of the patient's and the analyst's internal group dynamics, giving rise to an extended group situation. Corrao often said that there is no analysis between two people, but that each analysis involves a group instead. The group consists of the characters that emerge in the session, thanks to the joint creation by patient and analyst.

Finally, Corrao's unsaturated field, an encounter between the patient's and the analyst's internal group dynamics where narrative transformations are at work, has been fertilised by Bion, especially with regard to the dream. If you give me a few more weeks, I might even add a new advancement of the field, the fifth one, that of the *group dream-game*.

> So, if your way of working has progressed so much and is still constantly changing, I cannot but ask you, on behalf of the many analysts who are still seeking their own analytic voice, to tell us about how your thought changed throughout your career.

I think I have had many changes in my way of working. However, I keep changing following some tips that I get directly or indirectly from patients. For example, I remember when I was a Kleinian—*mon dieu*, I really was—and a patient came to me and said, "Now I have to have a serious talk with you. I have no intention of lying down on the couch, I have to tell you something really important instead. When I arrived in your office, I had a problem. That problem was my boyfriend. After I left at the end of the session, I found myself with two problems: one with my boyfriend, and the second one with you. I wonder, what was my mistake?"

This episode goes back to when I was Kleinian, and I interpreted everything transferentially. This event was very important to me, because it allowed me to distance myself from the obligation to continually interpret transference. It became important to me to highlight the transformations that occurred in the session, instead of translating immediately what the patient said about her boyfriend in a transference interpretation. This opened my mind to the idea that the most important thing was to transform the relationship of the patient with her boyfriend. But in my mind, the boyfriend was me, without a doubt.

Except, I no longer felt the need to remind the patient that the boyfriend was me.

> So sometimes a boyfriend is just a boyfriend?

Yes, for a long time the boyfriend was just the boyfriend, but in my mind—in the kitchen—it was me.

Many years later, when I arrived at the concept of the field, I developed another idea, namely that the boyfriend was a character in the field. So, there are the boyfriend, the patient's father, the dog. Every character is in the field. If the patient talks about something outside the field, for example "My cousin from Buenos Aires is a killer!", the field widens to include Buenos Aires and the killer. In my mind I think that the killer is in the office, and that we have to cook in order to digest him. For a long time, I do not know whether the killer is part of the patient or me. Everything is produced together, by both.

So, my idea of the field is that of the internal group that a patient brings with him, in the encounter with the internal group of the analyst that opens the office door. As soon as these groupalities meet, we have an immediate transformation of all of this in the field, inhabited by all these characters.

When a new character enters the field, I do not necessarily think that the character comes from the past or from external reality. I consider that, at this point, the field needs a character coming from the outside in order to express something. Of course I always keep in mind that the field acts as a global positioning system that allows us to continuously know where we are heading towards, and that we have to choose the direction that corresponds to the patient's needs or internal worlds, rather than to our own.

> You often called the field model a weak theory, but at other times it seems that you want to "field-ify" the whole world. How do you explain this apparent contradiction? And above all, what do you mean by weak theory?

Weak theory means a theory that preserves a large space for change, which foresees its transience and that has a strong fascination for the new and the unknown. Field theory foresees in some way its own extinction, foresees also a coveted desire to see, to know what comes next and, therefore, opens up to the future, opens up to the new, opens up to what we do not know; it is curious: in this sense the field is a weak model.

It's a strong model once you're within it, you get to know it, and to spend time with it: it becomes quite difficult to think as if Bion had never been born, or as if wolves did not exist, and as if we were ever at the origin of the study of the psyche. We know very little, however we've made a few little steps and we deserve to enjoy their fruits.

"Field-ify" the world, you say, but we mean the analytic world, because I still think that psychoanalysis outside the setting remains a great way of thinking, but it's like existentialism or Marxism. They are things that fascinate me, but that have very little to do with our profession. I only care about psychoanalysis as a discipline that relieves mental suffering. This is its specificity, this is the only thing that I think it's good for. If then somebody manages to use it instead of a jack to change their car's tyre, I have no objection, as long as they do not ask me to do it.

At the same time, I would not "field-ify" the world, in the sense of saying that the only thing that works is the field. The field is a great discovery, it is a great invention, a great model that will last for ten, twenty, thirty, maybe forty or fifty years, and the interesting thing will be seeing the evolution of the field. Since its birth, the concept of field has changed a lot: we are at least at the fourth generation of the concept. The first conceptualisation was the Barangers'; now it smells like a dusty attic. And along the way we had more variations that keep enabling new explorations. It's like the iPhone: I hope we'll see the iPhone 7, iPhone 8, iPhone 9 soon, and then there will be a leap in the model, and it will no longer be called iPhone: it will be called maybe Gamma 32, and then there will be the Gamma 33. A loud and clear point about psychoanalysis is that new models keep being developed and then there are new discoveries:

it is an expanding universe, a radically expanding universe. Models should be ever expanding; here instead—I'm using an old expression on purpose—there is a continuous castration of everything that is potentially new, because it is disturbing. So much so that Grotstein titled one of his best books, *Do I Dare Disturb the Universe?* (1981).

The analysts' universe does not want to be disturbed, it wants to slumber soundly, and psychoanalysis that used to be such a revolutionary, disruptive science, at one point has become in many cases a kind of general purpose antibiotic.

And so we get to a few questions about the analytic field, your now very famous model of work, with which one might try to disturb the universe. The analytic field is that field of unconscious forces formed by crossing the projective identifications of the two people in the office. Everything regarding the analysis of a patient is in the field, there is no "outside" in analysis. So far, so good. So I start with the question that many have asked themselves, but that maybe not many have asked you. In the clinical vignettes that you present in your work, you often relate phrases attributed to the characters as communications to the analyst. Let's see a few examples. "The other day the tyre dealer inflated my tyres too much," "My mother is so irritating when she puts her foot down." Ferro—so would casually comment a colleague who did not know your model too well—would read these sentences as referring to the analyst: the tyres that are too inflated are too active and saturated interventions, the irritating mother is the analyst who is overly pressing, in a perspective where everything is transference. For some this is all a bit too simple and a tad claustrophobic. Is it always you and me, I and you?

Donnel Stern wrote some absolutely likeable and smart things about this in his book *Relational Freedom*, published in 2015 by Routledge, which I hope will have an Italian edition soon. He tells parody stories about how I could have interpreted some communications: "If Ferro was in New

York and a patient told him he had eaten a hotdog, he would have understood ..." and there begins a game on the many narratable stories.

When I use vignettes in my texts, they are an attempt to communicate something that is impossible to communicate, because it is like trying to convey a recipe: when you write it down it loses its smell, warmth, temperature, right? So a narrated recipe is something that vaguely resembles the dish in its actuality. We owe the idea of transference as a total situation to Betty Joseph (1985) in the first place, so it is not even such an original idea, after all we already owe to Klein that everything that happens in the office relates to the internal world. Klein looked at the patient's internal world; the quantum leap was to realise that we have two internal worlds, and that transference as a total situation, of which I am absolutely convinced, is not just the one-way transference from the patient towards the analyst, despite it being prevalent—three motorway lanes out of four—but that at least one lane is being used in the opposite direction, from the analyst towards the patient. Let's add to this that other realities that have to do with the one or the other are being formed, and they are born from the encounter: after all it's the two of them in that office, so the most immediate thing is precisely what happens there in the office. So, whereas in a Kleinian perspective all of this would be continually explained, continuously interpreted, in a field perspective, all of this is being played as a game. Given these characters, today we are playing the tyre dealer who inflates tyres too much. It is not a given that the tyre dealer is the analyst and that the tyres are the patient's, that's the beauty of the field, being able not to ascribe, that is, that the annoying mother is me. Let's make a movie where there is an annoying mother. Who do we choose to direct it? Nanni Moretti? The same movie directed by Quentin Tarantino would be different. In Moretti's movie there would probably be ironic-comic-tragic notes. In Tarantino's movie the annoying mother ends up with her throat sliced open. There are a thousand possible developments: that is just the beginning. It's a movie that begins, say, with an intrusive mother or with a tyre dealer that inflates the tyres too much. Then we have a movie waiting to be shot, and it is not a given that the actor will be the one or the other. There may be a thousand ways to mask something and there may be a masked character whose identity we do not understand for a long time, we do not know if he has more to do with the analyst or with the patient, but it's still something under construction. Unlike Kleinianism, it makes no sense to say: "You are afraid that I'm filling you up too much with the things I say." In a field perspective this would be an outdated interpretation, it would be the end of the field. An interpretation of this kind would mean the collapse of the field and a return to a highly relational situation. A highly relational situation means you and me, I and you, within you, within me, I respond to you and you respond to me. A field situation means to let these characters live and play with them. We are in a village, there is a tyre dealer who inflates tyres too much, then word gets out, so we hand the story as we said to Nanni Moretti or Quentin Tarantino and see what movie comes out of it. We cannot know beforehand, the best part is doing it together, building it: where are we going to end up today? "Tonight we improvise," Pirandello would say.

Historically, psychoanalysis developed as a treatment for repression, which took away imaginative and emotional material from consciousness, with a kind of horizontal cut of consciousness. We might say, simplifying, that field theory is more focused on the development of the split and dissociated areas, seen as vertical cuts in consciousness?

I think that the phenomena of repression and the phenomena of splitting are certainly present in the analytic field, but somehow the repressed aspects, even the split aspects, are basically already there, already created. My split part is already one of my working parts, it is offstage but is right next to the theatre, right next to it in a shop, in an office nearby, but it already exists. What concerns us now and should concern us ever more is what has not yet reached the level of the thinkable, that is all that is upstream of the split, all that is still absolutely upstream of the alpha function.

> I have another question that I would like to ask, regarding listening to the patient's communications, an issue on which you are focusing attention. I will make a grotesque caricature of the situation here too. "The patient has a heater locked on maximum heat, and he feels a terrible heat at home." OK, so I, a new analyst, understand that I am too close, so I draw away a bit, maybe I stay silent a bit. "The repair man came and fixed it but now the bidet water is a bit too cold." Well, I'm too far away. I should be a bit warmer, it's time to talk. And so on. Isn't there is a risk that, if one is not named Ferro, he'll unconsciously end up continually colluding with the patient's unconscious requests?

I'll say two things: first, that obliging the patient's unconscious request seems all well and good, for a while. I do not see why we should not satisfy the patient too: let him get what he wants, poor thing, as long as it makes sense and as long as it is made explicit in the game of the field. Here, the second point is important. I repeat that we should leave behind the idea that the field is you and me, or rather the "you and me" according to which more warmth is needed, so I get close, or more cold is needed, so I draw away; it is still within a post-Kleinian relational perspective: you and me, I and you. So, maybe what is so hard to convey in the books is the complexity of the field, because, for example, one is forced to say, "Then I thought ... then I moved away ... but then the bidet was cold ... so I got close ..." and so on. Unfortunately it's not like this, because we are still in a relational perspective, whereas in a field perspective I should be able to say, "Let's make a good movie—and have Hitchcock direct it; no, today we let Charlie Chaplin direct it—where there is a story with a bidet that does not work and a heater that's too hot," and see what happens. But all this happens without there being a need to go to meet the patient's desire, except in terms of promoting an atmosphere that allows transformations. It is very difficult to get out of the post-Klein, because post-Klein *à la* Betty Joseph is very compelling for us analysts, but it is also very fracturing for the patient. Whereas if we transform the analytic situation from an interpretive situation to a transformative situation and, I insist, a playful situation, it turns out that today we're playing plumbers. Today we play with the heater that does not work, today we play with the cold bidet. How many things might orbit around a cold bidet, if that Venetian director gets his hands on it, what's his name? Tinto Brass![1] In a movie titled *Cold Bidets*, Tinto Brass would have Claudia Koll washing herself in a bidet, while another director would put on the cold bidet the friar from *Miracle of Marcelino*, who had to use a cold bidet because the monastery had no money.

> It seems clear to me that the field works through directorial transformations that gradually give life to the movie, Tarantino-style, Moretti-style. But how do you decide who the director is in a given scene?

The directors too are characters who arise from the mental lives of analyst and patient, and maybe with a certain degree of vigilance, we realise that if there is a patient who is always giving work to the director of *Miracle of Marcelino*, a bit of Tinto Brass is needed here. It is part of that activity of introduction of the characters, the *casting* function, because the function of director is part of the characters too.

Maybe I would say that there is an asymmetry in place. There are two *loci* of asymmetry, whereas the analytic situation is quite symmetrical, despite what they say. One place of asymmetry is ethical responsibility. There's no fooling around it, the ethical responsibility of what happens in an office is the analyst's, 99.999 periodical per cent. This is the area of greatest asymmetry. I believe that there is also a second situation of asymmetry, in the fact that the analyst should know that, under his jacket, he wears on his shirt the insignia of captain, so he is responsible for setting the course. The responsibility, thus, is asymmetrical, and I think that the analyst's possibility to be the one who governs the directors is part of this responsibility. The choice of director belongs to the patient too, to the couple, but a bit of asymmetry is in order: if there is an overly prudish patient at some point someone has to introduce Tinto Brass, or a story *à la* Tinto Brass. And who has to go get Tinto Brass? After a while it may be that the patient introduces him, but if the patient, after years, has not introduced Tinto Brass yet, the analyst can go to fetch this character. Not all characters need be introduced by the patient. A good number of characters are snapshots taken by the patient of the analyst, or of the field, but the analyst too may introduce his characters in a thousand different ways: he may introduce them with a "I was thinking about a movie I saw yesterday ...", he may introduce them with a reverie, he may introduce them with a "I remember that when I was young my uncle ...", making up what his uncle did out of whole cloth, or he may also introduce them with a particular attitude to directorial change. And so we come back to what was about playing a game: I think that analysis should be as much of a game situation as possible.

Having come this far, I think that making the transition from child analysis, that actually uses this type of activity much more often, is much more understandable.

In child analysis the analyst plays games.

> Perhaps what the analyst in training or even the fully trained analyst is concerned about—rightly so I think—is avoiding occupying too much of the field, making his characters, who may derive from his "Tinto Brass" inclination, overly present. The abstinent analyst runs less of a danger, while the analyst that inserts characters and is responsible for directing, runs the risk to give rise to anti-therapeutic interventions or, more generally, to cause an invasion of the patient's space.

Sure, an analyst who always puts in Tinto Brass would be a depressed analyst, someone who looks for a way to be excited in therapy, or one who always puts in Tinto Brass or Quentin Tarantino; the analyst should have a roster of characters and directors approaching infinity. Somehow the analyst becomes the co-producer, a co-producer who has a wide selection of which actors to engage through casting and which director to use. It is obvious that the patient is entitled to the same choice, and the aim is to develop the patient's discourse and not our own.

It's as if, thinking about the game of Lego, the patient could also use those Lego bits that can only be used in one specific way, such as the firefighter or the gas pump. On the other hand the analyst should mainly use those Lego pieces that are used to make more connections, except if there is a story that got stuck because it lacks a firefighter, then I cannot see why the analyst should not put the firefighter in that story.

> One wonders how much otherness can the patient endure.

The patient or the analyst?

And I thought that was going to be easy. I would start from the patient, then maybe we can deal with the analyst.

Enduring otherness is not easy, because they are all potential identities; for this reason the concept of field is useful: because we are not just two; when we meet with the patient we are two, after a fraction of a second we are four, after two seconds we are six, soon we are seventy-two people in the office. And the field is accounting for this whole complex group situation that is generated. And playing with this group situation, being able to transform this group situation. But now you are going to ask me, the signals we get from the field, to what extent are we to follow them?

As it happens, that was exactly what I was going to ask you.

We analysts are students for a long time, because analytic training does not last four years but many more, and it is quite tragic that the average age of the analyst has increased, meaning that one starts working as an independent analyst at the age of fifty, sixty years. Because the time needed for studying is long. So, as long as anyone is a student he is in great need of signals from the field—I have always used the metaphor of the global positioning system as something that gives us signals about the state of the field—and more-over the global positioning system's signals are multiplying, because each group or subgroup of characters gives us its different indication or signalling; so we have a group, a field of global positioning systems. So, when the analyst finally manages to be less of a student and can make a leap, there is that wonderful leap by which the analyst, from being an aspiring scientist, turns to the role of aspiring artist, so there is no more need for signals from the field, there's just going by instinct without any map, without a compass, manag-ing to create with the patient a highly creative, highly fertile couple. Keep in mind that it takes forty years to get there, it is like a pianist who plays masterfully with no score, or plays jazz with sounds as yet unwritten. There are forty years of practice behind that. Eugenio Gaburri would say that this is the time when Dersu Uzala[2] takes the place of the cartographer.

> Many answers in this book call for creativity and flair on the analyst's part. Should a new analyst take these points as the basis of his professional career, and gallop full speed on the prairie, or keep them in a corner of the mind, kneading them into his West Point, waiting to master the technique needed to give a solid foundation to creative inspiration?

I think that creativity and inspiration are the finish line: alas, one always needs to start from West Point, just like how at school we have to start from the ABCs, from the fundamentals. Then there's a long journey, a long journey made of study, a long journey made of supervision, a long journey made of meetings and clashes with colleagues. And all of this brings us towards our possible artistic dimension.

I remember how my high school teacher corrected a sentence a very bright classmate of mine had used, and he protested explaining that the same expression had been used by Leopardi or maybe Foscolo,[3] and the teacher then said: "Yes, but you are not a poet! Or at least, not yet!"

Here, I think you have to reach the level of the artistic simplicity of poetry to be able to dispose of all grammar, all syntax; but the journey to do this is long and certainly exhausting.

As Edison once said, in order to be truly creative you need one per cent inspiration and ninety-nine per cent perspiration. I think that we all need to sweat, to have sweated, and to keep sweating, because only then can one truly achieve those summits of creative art that will repay all the effort that has been made over the decades. So, I am not talking about a simplification or an easy invention at all, but about achieving what for a pianist might be an act of virtuosity, a creative or interpretive capacity of a text, forgetting grammar, syntax, grids, global positioning systems, but it is the culmination of a great and hard labour.

> There is another aspect that I think is important. The fact that the field breathes, expands and contracts until sometimes it collapses. It expands with the development of new narratives, new characters ...

I'd like to highlight that the stories should always be consistent with the internal world of both, the analyst should not start making movies on his own.

> I think it is important that you highlight the relevance of the stories, to be clear. So there is a four-hand expansion, and then at some point the field has to contract with a kind of selected fact: for example, I'm thinking about transference interpretations or something that narrows down a bit the number of possible stories. Could you explains when—assuming it makes sense to make generalisations about this operation, at least in theory—the field should expand and when it might make sense to have it contract?

We could take a few examples from literature: when does a writer introduce a new character? When did Alessandro Manzoni introduce Father Cristoforo?[4] The moment he is introduced is sublime. Without Father Cristoforo the story would be lost, it would flake apart. Father Cristoforo's entrance strongly reorganises the narrative, so every time the narrative is about to flake apart, there enters a strong character that allows the narrative to go back to being alive and fascinating. So this choice is difficult to share, it is not scientifically transmissible. You need an artistic flair here, there's no helping that. The analyst is like a novelist, except that our novels last the space of fifty minutes, which is a shame, because we write wonderful novels: oftentimes the sessions are unique pieces of fiction. It is like cooking: you make a wonderful dish, yes, you can reconstruct the recipe afterwards, but a recipe that only vaguely recalls the dish you just cooked. Same with analysis, it is not reproducible with hard rules in a planned way. How does Manzoni, how does Dostoyevsky bring that character, that action into the scene? You let the patient steer you somewhat, thankfully, the patient continually gives you suggestions, but when do you bring Abbot Busoni into the scene? And when does revenge, the Count of Monte Cristo, enter? Here is the magic of narratives and how to interrupt them, how to develop them, how to change them completely. I think that we will hone the tools through which to expand our imagination thanks to writers, thanks to the rhythm of writing or thanks to directors, which is what we did for years with *infant observation*, crucial because it got us in touch with all the primitive fantasies in the mother–child couple. Is analysis the reproduction of the mother–child couple, though? Absolutely not, so much so that analysts of importance such as André Green, Francesco Corrao, and others always said that infant observation was as good as the observation of a retiree sitting on a bench; whatever we observe develops some capacity, so the observation of the great classics of literature would open up a number of tools, of worlds, of perspectives, and of narrative devices.

Notes

1. Translator's note: Italian filmmaker Tinto Brass is mostly known for his erotic movies. Actress Claudia Koll starred in his most successful movie, *All Ladies Do It*.
2. *Dersu Uzala* is a movie directed by Akira Kurosawa in which a group of Siberian explorers meets an old nomadic hunter, at first considered rude and eccentric, then praised for his intelligence, his powers of observation, his insight and his humanity.

3. Giacomo Leopardi and Ugo Foscolo are famous Italian poets of the nineteenth century.

4. Father Cristoforo is a character in Alessandro Manzoni's seminal nineteenth-century novel *I promessi sposi* (*The Betrothed*). An energetic friar with a troubled past and a fiery temper, Cristoforo defies the local lord, the wicked Don Rodrigo, in order to rescue the protagonist Lucia from his clutches.

CHAPTER EIGHT

Technical issues

You're talking about the artist's touch, instinct, a bit of nose. How much do you have to think before speaking in analysis, if you are an analyst?

Well, if you are the patient it is instantaneous: you just speak. Being the patient is much easier. The patient does not know what he's doing. Ideally we should have an analyst who is like the patient, who can speak and say what his heart suggests to him, or what his rhinencephalon suggests to him, or what emotion suggests to him, but I think those are acts of virtuosity that happen in one session per year.

Indeed, the analyst should at least in small part be oriented to resort even to the so-called negative capability, that ability to know how to wait in order to understand, introducing the minimum number of characters needed to move the story a little forward. It's like shooting a film of an American highway running straight through the desert; a few hours after the car stopped in the middle of the desert, an analyst might introduce a donkey, another introduces a cow, another introduces a gas station. The session has to be dressed, even with the introduction of characters that will then allow the expansion, the development of something. And one thing I would highlight is how all of this serves to allow things of which we are not aware to come out. That is, our point of interest is always that which is not yet known, which is unconscious, or which will be built with the unconscious, though the term unconscious is one of those words which, despite having been abused, we will have to use, I think, for many decades yet. I hope that in a few decades we will find an even more suggestive, stronger word; however, today and surely tomorrow, and for the next five years, I think we will have to be the masters of the unconscious, or of the unconscious' formation. That is not a word, a concept of which we can get rid, whether it is meant in one way or the other, accounting for the fact that Freud interprets it in one way, Klein in another way, Bion in a completely different way still; let's just say that it is a cursed area that is relevant to us.

The unconscious: place or function of the mind?

Function. Without a doubt. There is a word that Civitarese (2014) invented, *inconsciare*,[1] that also has a bit of sexuality reminiscent of the thighs,[2] so as a word it is full of references, even sensual-erotic, passional-Freudian ones. This word is beautiful because this is our problem, how can we manage to *inconsciare*. This is our future. I think Civitarese defines it very well: building and training the unconscious was Bion's idea, nonetheless Civitarese was able to define, with that neologism, what we really should be doing in our work: being able to *inconsciare* communications, missed communications. That is, *inconsciare* and dreaming are our goals, or *inconsciare* through dreaming. There is a continuous back and forth that exists in Bion, in post-Bion, between dream, dreamlike, and the unconscious, which is something we still have to sift through. And it is unfortunate when instead of sifting through these things, we go about saying, "Yes, in 1922 Freud … the Two Principles …": it really is an immense loss. It's like going to a museum instead of taking the *Star Trek* spaceship and going towards unexplored spaces. We can still go to the museum, there is always time to go to the museum, but, between taking the *Star Trek* spaceship and going to another galaxy and going into blacks holes, going to other worlds, between that and going to the Louvre ... Well, the Louvre is beautiful, but we can still visit it when we are retired; let's explore as long as we can go and explore other worlds, other places, other non-places. We should be great explorers, not entomologists.

> This idea of exploration suggests a journey into the unknown. So, when a new analyst moves between the many things that he does not know, he feels his sense of responsibility weighing more heavily on him: it comes down to selecting which track to follow, because I could do countless opening speeches. One wonders what paths could lead the patient to a place where it makes sense to go, to help him. I'm thinking about how dangerous flying by the seat of your pants is; my fear is that—by saying something—I am acting out. An analyst who lacks forty years of experience and want to be a virtuoso might end up stepping on his patient's toes, imagining they're having a nice trip together while the patient feels abused.

There was an old article, I don't remember its author, that talked about the positive effect of misinterpretations. So we should not think that an incorrect intervention or a micro-action are indelible stains; we need an attitude more like Father Cristoforo's *omnia munda mundis*;[3] if an analyst does something with a pure soul, it is not a great sin. I know of very few analyses that were ruined because the analyst said one word more or one less. I think that the important point is that the analyst should be pure of heart to put it like Father Cristoforo would, when he says *omnia munda mundis*. Everything is pure to pure people, and the patient knows very well if the analyst is crooked, a scoundrel, or a liar, or a corruptor, or if he has a clean heart. The patient knows this, perceives this, and is absolutely conscious of this, so I would not worry that much about a technical error; if one makes a technical error, he can fix it. Even a painter can adjust his painting if there's a smear. In that painting there is that lady's bag that came out really bad, but the rest is beautiful, it carries the atmosphere of New York in January, at 3 pm, as it starts to get dark, and it's less than 20° C, that's New York. OK, so the lady's bag came out wrong, but it does not affect the picture at all.

Too many times analysts devote themselves to trifling details, I don't want to be offensive but I think that we keep looking at oligophrenic details, as in Rorschach,[4] while we should always look for the "global response with colour" of how a situation works. Who speaks first, who speaks second, keeping a twenty-five minutes' silence with the patient, they all look foolish things to me. Tugs of war, establishing who is dominant in the couple, "I get to make the rules here", what's the point?

> At this point if you discredit silence too, you deserve a question! Theoretically speaking, the analyst's silence facilitates that state of regression, that derailment of conscious thought that makes it so that the primary thought emerges more easily, and thus desire, slip of the tongue, transference, and everything else that used to be kept at bay. What's your opinion?

I'll answer in a roundabout way: I think I derail only when I have a reverie and it happens quite often to me, given how I function mentally. I'm not an analyst with a low frequency of reverie. My functioning is such that sometimes several images appear to me in one session, and then using them is not always as easy as in the example I used before. Oftentimes the meaning remains a bit mysterious, sometimes you have to work on it; reverie, to describe it in old-fashioned language, is a kind of micro-dream of countertransference done in the session. And another derailment that I have experienced is when I fall asleep. It is very important if one falls asleep, because if one falls asleep, and does not come from a sleepless night, then the patient's defence, with which he put his monsters to sleep, put lions and cheetahs to sleep, is really starting to crumble. It no longer is so cocooned, "opium is taking effect", and the defence of sleep that so far the patient has used against his proto-emotions is manifesting in the field; it now infects the analyst, so that the anaesthetised analyst falls asleep too. This is the first phase in order to be able then to wake up, to rouse from their sluggish and sleepy state cheetahs, tigers, or whatever else, that until that moment had to be hibernated. So, sleep actually is the time when hibernating becomes a shared phenomenon, and from there you begin to "de-hibernate" the situation. Outside of that, I think I'm always relatively vigilant, because in the end it is the patient that stages everything there is to stage, with my cooperation too, so there is no particular secret that needs to get out, to jump out. Otherwise we return to a view of the unconscious as something pre-established, that is already there, that is a piece of the patient's mind that I have to allow to emerge. We play with the unconscious, we build it, we do it on our own day by day through the game that we play with the split parts, with the parts that manifest in session. What's important is analytic listening: there is a dream of a patient who was really inhibited, and at some point she encountered a person walking down the stairs to my office, a very sensual blonde woman with a skirt. Who is this character though? We let her walk down the stairs, why should we care who walks down the stairs? It is obvious that the patient is bringing into the field an aspect of this fascinating, sensual woman in a skirt, with which she cannot identify yet. So maybe it's a split part of the self. Later one could say, and here I am joking, "What colour was that woman's hair though?", knowing full well that the patient is blonde too. Or you could play, asking where does this mysterious woman come from, we do not know, but the moment this beautiful woman wearing lipstick and a sexy skirt walks in, there is another character in the office, telling you about living, fundamental aspects, with whom maybe a new movie kicks off, such as *The Seven Year Itch* with Marilyn Monroe. Each character who comes in opens up new possible rooms in what too often was described as a Way of the Cross—I do not know why there is this whole mystique of pain—that is, in analysis.

Of course there is pain, in life there is pain too, but we should not idealise pain as a good aspect, on which to dwell for as long as possible, because we already have so much pain in separations, in estrangements, in death, in diseases—knocking on wood here—so let's try to do other things in analysis too. Analysis should be a pleasure, it should be a game but also a game where you play as in De Filippo's theatre,[5] where you often play with tragic themes. Think of *These Ghosts* or *Filumena Marturano*; however you play it, theatre is a game. And analysis is a form of game, there's not much more to say about it. It would be better to share, to allow the patient the pleasure of the game, that operation performed by Benigni in his movie about Auschwitz, *Life is Beautiful*, which was heavily criticised and many found horrible, monstrous. I think that Benigni's idea, managing to make the idea of a monstrous thing tolerable to a child, was brilliant. You have to know how to play a game: that is a very serious thing, and deeply ethical in my opinion.

If I think about *Life is Beautiful*, which I really liked, I wonder how a child like the one in the movie could have actually digested a reality so masked as to have its emotional meaning completely distorted, albeit in a seemingly positive way.

Our mental life though allows us to survive even when it is completely mystified: defences are lies, lies are mystifications. If we stop to think that at any given moment we might have a ruptured aneurysm, all the misfortunes that might happen, from an acute meningitis to a heart attack, to a tumour, we would just lie on the bed and stay still forever. So we defend ourselves with omnipotence, with denial. A right mix of these things allows us to live, to be happy, because we just bought some pasta for dinner.

> Since we are talking about heart attacks and tumours, I'm getting anxious, so let's get back to the problem of silence.

Silence.

I do not see why we have to be silent, except if there is a moment of intense communication, which may also exist, a poetic moment of silence. But I can't stand an analyst who is silent for silence's sake! I had referred the daughter of a colleague to another colleague, with whom she was very uncomfortable; she then came back after six months with this request: "Tell me the name of another analyst, as long as he can speak." She wanted an analyst who said something, who would get involved in the discussion. Here, the silent analyst is a sphinx, he is made of stone, he is like one of those statues that you find in the gardens of Rome. Be alive!

> In Bologna, Glauco Carloni said that an analyst is more likely to regret speaking up than being silent.

Of course an analyst that doesn't speak much says less nonsense than one who speaks a lot, but we should cut some slack to nonsense. Among many things that one says, some may be nonsense, others may be not.

> However, it is also true that if you say fewer things, they may be heard more. They are more precious.

Two uncles of mine once left for a trip together; they travelled from Palermo to Naples. Without exchanging a word. Once in Naples, they climbed up the Vomero hills and one of them, looking at the gulf from above, made this gesture (extends his arm, as if to show the gulf lying in front of him) and the other replied with this other gesture (as if to say: "wonderful ..."). After this exchange, they went back from Naples to Palermo without uttering another word. Is that OK? If they liked it, well, why not? Life is short though, there are so many things we could tell each other, let's talk!

Notes

1. Translator's note: Inconsciare is a verb driven from inconscio (Eng. unconscious). We can translate it as to unconsciate.
2. Translator's note: Untranslatable play on the words *inconsciare* (unconsciate) and *cosce* (It. thighs).
3. Latin: "To the pure all things are pure."
4. In the Rorschach test scoring system, an oligophrenic detail is defined as a response in which a part of the stimulus is seen when one would expect the whole to be seen.
5. Translator's note: Eduardo De Filippo (1900–1984) was an Italian actor and playwright. His plays often merged drama with farce. *These Ghosts* and *Filumena Marturano* are two of his best-known works.

CHAPTER NINE

Dreaming

And so we get to the dream, at last. Freud—and on this we agree—taught us that the dream plays an important role in our internal world. Today, for every ten analysts, you will find eleven different ways to interpret dreams. The dream depicts the patient's internal world, signals his unconscious desires, his way of relating with others, represents his relationship with the analyst, or the analysis phase he is going through. It gives shape to that which cannot be represented.

In this maze, it seems that contemporary psychoanalysis is shifting the focus from the latent content of the dream to the manifest content. Indeed, the widely held habit of asking associations to the dream is currently being questioned. Is there "work in progress" along the Royal Road to the unconscious?

Since we have to start from the past to understand Ogden I would like to mention Calderón de la Barca's *Life is a Dream*. I would say that the whole analytic session is a dream, because a session of analysis moves from the assumption—as Aldo Costa, Francesco Corrao's first pupil, who should not be forgotten, said—that the first bereavement the analyst has to go through is the bereavement of reality. From the moment you are in analysis, indeed, everything the patient says is not to be considered as a reality, in any case.

I believe that the dream is really the last thing that should be interpreted, but that it is something to play with. There are dreams, for example, in which there is little to interpret. There is a brilliant surgeon, in analysis four sessions a week, who has a dream. He is someone who keeps his chin up with a drug, that is younger and younger women, to try to stem the pain that after the forties come the forty-fives and then the fifties, the fifty-fives, which is not a pretty thing and each one struggles to manage it. There are those who would buy a Porsche and those like him who resort to this expedient, to have these young women, younger and younger—now he got to the "twenty-somethings". And he has this dream, which I found really amazing, since he has this very young lover. The dream is that he was performing surgery, however in the peritoneal sac there were blackberries, and these blackberries were then filtered and out came a peculiar liquid; by giving this blackberry juice to some desperate children, these children stopped crying. Do we have to bring who knows what into this to understand this dream? I was tempted to ask him at once: "Is Stella blonde-haired or black-haired?", but guessing can also be dangerous. So I waited until later in the session before asking him this question, when Stella turned up again in the session. He replied that she was black-haired, so a clear "Ha ha!" was enough, and that was the interpretation of the dream. The meaning is that the blackberry was used to make the children stop crying, but the dream is so self-evident that there is no need to interpret it.

Obviously there is also a theoretical reason for all of this, but for now I would say that the dream is like a child's game, it is already very advanced. We do not start by learning to handle clay, knead it, make a toy soldier, then take more clay, shape the bayonet, put it in the hands of the soldier and then build the Indian; the dream has already evolved, we are already dealing with the Indian and the soldier fighting. The hardest part is the first one: finding the clay, finding the colours with which to paint the Indians, taking some more clay; this is everything that comes before. The dream is the last part, when all these processes have already been made upstream thanks to the alpha function, from the senses to pictograms. And then the dream is when the dish is already there, done and cooked, so there is no need to interpret it, it's ready-to-serve. Children stop crying when they get a blackberry, what more do I have to say? Why not? "Maybe a red berry would work as well—one might add—it doesn't have to be a blackberry!", but it's pretty obvious.

Psychoanalysis is a simple thing, that we psychoanalysts for a long time have been trying to make as complicated and obscure as possible, like the Orphic-Pythagorean mysteries. Psychoanalysis is a process of a terrific simplicity: it talks about how we, being together, can metabolise the brutality of reality. That's what the primitive tribes mentioned by Devereux[1] did, when in the evening they began to tell dreams, to tell stories. This allowed the working through of reality.

> So, if I am not mistaken, you think that the heart of the psychoanalytic process is the expansion of the capacity for dreaming of the couple, to allow the patient to acquire the tools for an increased metabolisation of reality?

Nowadays the focus is on the dream: this aspect is essential. Let me give you an example. I meet a supervisee, I usually ask: "So, how are you?" It is a very generic question, he says that he went to Naples and Pompeii. "We went up Mount Vesuvius with a jeep, the jeep was bouncing around wildly, we went just next to Mount Vesuvius' crater and there was smoke coming out, and then there were these weird Neapolitans who spoke an incomprehensible language, it was all Arab to me, I did not understand a word. Talking in English with someone who knew it was easier than understanding Neapolitan." After some small talk, the supervisee goes on to tell me about the session with his patient. It's a fairly dull session, a session in which the patient keeps talking about children. The patient was a lot like the example I gave earlier, her aunt is a nun, she is a kindergarten teacher, and that basically they talked for the longest time about children, poo, pee, nappies, in short, all of these aspects of events regarding children.

So, if we think that the dream status pertains not only to the analysis situation, but pertains to any work situation of analysis, and thus to supervision too, if we consider everything that's inside the supervision frame—what may appear as a session about nothing but children, where one peed, another one pooed—as a communication to the supervisor, I believe that the supervisee is saying that together with the patient we began approaching a hot area, Mount Vesuvius, we started to get close to a place where there are people who speak a strange language, an incomprehensible language, so it seems we moved from the north of the world with its Pampers nappies, to this completely chaotic Arab world where you do not understand the language. There is a complete equivalence between the analysis session and the supervision session, so everything begins from the first communication, when the patient comes in and says that yesterday he went there and this happened, a discourse of simple chatter. If we consider all of that as the field, then it is supervision from the moment we open the door to the moment we say goodbye to the patient.

In this way we play on the specific strength of analysis, that is the dream; consistently with Ogden, we say that the essential function of the analytic work is exactly to be able to turn into a dream, meaning in a narration that is then shared, everything that is pressing there as a symptom, such as anxiety, such as malaise, such as split aspects. So if we imagine a sheet of paper torn into a hundred pieces, and we put these hundred pieces into the liver, then a hypochondria of having a liver disease is developed. If on the other hand we manage to glue these pieces together, we make a whole sheet and read it, the liver is cured and we know what the sheet is talking about. So the point I would start from is that it was the analysts who turned analysis into a very complicated thing, because it really is a very simple thing, you just need to keep thinking. Once we are with the patient, it is in our best interest, in his best interest to communicate, it suffices not to keep accusing him that everything is his fault, that he attacks, misunderstands, is envious. Just imagine if we met a friend who wanted to talk to us and we told him: "You are resisting, you are envious, you attack the setting, you have some resistance ..." So I would start from this point, the simplicity of analysis and how it is being complicated to the point that there are words that I, after forty years in this line of work, do not yet know how to pronounce. I know how to pronounce *àpres-coup* in French, not in German. Why do we have to make an issue over-complicated? Let's call it re-signification. We like not being understood.

Not long ago, Thomas Ogden widened the idea of interpretation, from uttering an interpretation to the interpretive function of an unstructured conversation.

Talking-as-dreaming.

Exactly, talking-as-dreaming. What are, in your opinion, the risks and opportunities to be aware of in this kind of approach?

The risk is that the patient is cured, that he feels better, and that one way of making analysis is replaced by another one.

All right!

The risk, that is, really exists for the Terracotta Army, if it turns out they have a recorder inside that keeps repeating the same things. After all the greatest phobia is agoraphobia, it is thinking.

We are a species that does not want to think, even though the newest function of our species is thought. Vomiting, defecating, much less evolved species already do that. Thinking is the newest function of our species, and that is what we do not want to do, so we suffer from agoraphobia. What is agoraphobia? It is the fear of thinking, it is the fear of open spaces, it is the fear of what we do not know.

I recently read about an Italian scientist who, thanks to the discovery of twin pulsar stars, had shown that Einstein's theory was correct to 99.95 per cent. The researcher added that the scientific interest of the discovery was in that 0.05 per cent that didn't fit: what was behind that imperfection? What other perspectives? What new theories?

However, we analysts sometimes would like be claustrophobic, we would like to be always protected by our perfect theories that always add up, we would like to be able to stay inside our office, within which we are in a state of divinity. Thus forgetting that when we do get out …

And it is also for this reason that we would like to use psychoanalysis as a crowbar against all realities, to try not to have this experience of smallness. We are convinced that we are more important than orthopaedists, for example, or dermatologists or plumbers.

On the contrary we do a job like any other, which happens to be useful with respect to mental suffering. About this we really do know more than an orthopaedist.

Since we are talking about Ogden's dream theory, the author holds that even when the analyst is involved in the patient's dream, the dream is after all the patient's. How can I tell if I'm appropriating the patient's dream or movie?

I have a special fondness for Ogden, but I do not fully agree with this statement of his, in the sense that the patient's dream is always somehow polluted, we could even say supported, enriched by something belonging to the phantasmic life and creativity of the analyst. There are missing bits that the analyst compensates for; there is no doubt that an honest enough analyst should allow the patient to achieve his dream as much as possible, to dream and to enact those changes that regard his own life and his own stories. I think that a certain degree of contamination between the two minds is absolutely unavoidable, even desirable I would say.

> This answer raises another question. The difference between psychoanalysis and psychotherapy once used to be described with the metaphor of sixteenth-century artists, so that analysis worked by subtracting, like the sculptors that "removed" marble to make statues, as opposed to working by adding, as in the case of clay sculpting. In this way, it was suggested that the analyst should not add anything of his own within the patient. Now, leaving aside the fact that this partition looks quite idealised and unrealistic, we can not but think that, when someone says that the analyst fertilises the patient's mind, he is describing a very different operation from the one a textbook analyst would do.

I would say two things. I realise that I'm always giving roundabout answers because it seems to me that responding directly to the answer has a blocking effect; so it seems more productive to use the question to blaze a tangential trail that will, perhaps, bring us back to a kind of answer.

The first thing I would say, and I do not want to pass up the opportunity to say it, is that I would really love it if analysts learned more and more how to say: "I do not know this ... This is unclear to me ... We do not know this yet." And I am referring to the difference between psychoanalysis and psychotherapy too. One could mention, if not thousands, hundreds of theories about it. I would say that there is some difference, but I cannot say which difference yet, and I like to say "yet" because there is this idea that one day we will know more, and when we will know this thing there will still be many other things that we will not know.

And this theme goes hand in hand with another one, that is, healing factors. We do not know what the healing factors are, or rather, we got to know a few and so I would consider absolutely valid the list that we do know, starting from making unconscious … from making conscious what was unconscious.

You see, I'm already making a slip, maybe because the actual healing operation is to make unconscious what is overly conscious, that is to transform an overly concrete reality into a reality that can be dreamt; then there are all the other factors that we know. But I think that what should interest us the most are the non-specific healing factors.

What do I mean by non-specific healing factors? Do non-specific healing factors exist? No, they do not exist at all, they are all those aspects that we do not know what they consist of: in session we perform dozens of mental operations of which we know nothing, operations we perform unawarely and unknowingly, a bit like how could be done with projective identifications before Klein. It is obvious that projective identifications existed since the dawn of time, but from Klein onwards we recognised and identified them, and the same goes for all those non-specific healing factors that exist and that allow Kleinian, Freudian, Ogdenian analyses to work more or less in the same way. Of course, the fact remains that we do not know what these factors are, and we need all the time of clinical research to give a name and a status to these particular aspects.

So we go back to the original question …

Right, I was asking about the analyst's fertilisation of the mind.

I would say that regarding this aspect I would call into play genetics, that is, yes maybe you could even clone a child, but it would not be the best gift to give him. I do not know if I would use the expression that the analyst "fertilises", somehow it seems too active a role. I think the analyst uses tools that help creativity, participates in the atmosphere, makes a given atmosphere possible, allows himself fantasies, opens obstructed senses, walks paths that had been clogged up by undergrowth, paths that had become impassable. But I believe there is always a co-construction, a co-narrative, I would say, a co-being-able-to-dream of analyst and patient. The analysis, that is, is the result of two minds, and as such it would seem very unlikely to think of a mental life that developed without dusting itself, in varying measure, with the analyst's flour.

> And where does the analyst's flour come from? From free-floating attention, some would say. Oftentimes, when I enter a free-floating state, a subtle performance anxiety overtakes me. Am I following the patient's text too closely? Am I a bit too distracted? Am I filtering things through theory? I'm getting terribly bored: just let this session end! How much should this free-floating attention float, anyway?

I think that free-floating attention belongs to a different paradigm. Now that we understand the session in terms of field, in terms of dream field, the analyst's mental functioning has to be more dreaming, a functioning that is able to combine the *dreaming ensemble* in the sense of dreaming together, with the *dreaming ensemble* in the sense of putting to work inside the field all the various modes of dream that we have: the transformations in dream, the transformations in game, and considering the entire session as a dream; so our mental functioning has to be, I would say, that of attention—because the patient should be listened to, we have to be attentive to his communications—but such as to allow a certain softness, a receptivity of listening. So, I would consider this type of listening not so much like a Swiss cheese with holes in listening, which is somewhat of a risk with free-floating attention, but more like a sheep ricotta whey cheese, the fresh kind you can knead, soft and receptive, but that needs a fork or a spoon in order to be functional. So

I think that many concepts, including that of free-floating attention, should begin to occupy our display cabinets, like certain surgical tools of the past adorn the cabinets of a surgeon or a dentist.

> During my training I was repeatedly told that we should preferably use the patient's own metaphors. A bit by choice, a bit by chance, I started to rephrase the patient's speech more and more frequently by offering him metaphors that his speech evoked in me. I realise that maybe these are not reverie, they are simple scenes or images but perhaps are useful in portraying, in seeing things from another point of view, in fostering the ability to dream. So, I would like to ask you what is, in your opinion, the point of offering metaphors, and how can this activity be useful.

I think that 70 per cent of the analytic work is what you just described; there is no greater nonsense than to say that we should only use the patient's metaphors. It's Nonsense, with a capital N, because otherwise we could never bring anything new that the patient needs; so our metaphorising work, our interpretive work I would say too, is carried by metaphors that sometimes are mere metaphors rather than *reverie*, because they are very close to our consciousness and concern something of which we are quite aware. On the other hand, the metaphor can begin to convey something of which we are unaware, so that it looks more like the reverie; I believe that a metaphor always stands on two legs, one closer to a purer metaphor that concerns something that we know and that we turn into images, and the other closer to reverie that happens when we do not know and are not aware of something and we turn it into images. In any case the great majority of our interventions are reformulations through metaphors or through *reverie*—sometimes in a mixed way—of what the patient tells us, making it possible to bring the patient's speech to a different level of awareness, of de-concretising, of abstraction. If we consider Bion's grid—I apologise for the jargon—we work to facilitate transformations from beta to other dimensions.

And I think the analyst's work is basically this; obviously, if I tell the story of the Little Match Girl to each patient that walks in, this is not a metaphor, nor a story, this is a blocking analyst: do not tell everybody the tale of Thumbelina!

It has to be a story of something that came to life inside the office, that was born for the first time inside the office and it would be better not to use it too many times: the metaphor, *reverie*, or intervention has to be alive each time. The third time the same thing is repeated, even the office walls grumble.

So you say that analysis is a way to transform the ways of being of the patient or of the analytic couple—the characters that spring to life in the encounter—by building images and thus stories that make working through possible. Care to give an example?

The Little Match Girl! The anxieties that are vividly described in the story, *The Little Match Girl* are a place of the mind in which coexist abandonment, loneliness, sadness, pain, despair, which can then evolve into other possible stories. It might be a useful exercise: fill the narrative segment that is found between the anxieties of the Little Match Girl and a drug addict, a sex addict, a prostitute, a Red Brigades member, a fundamentalist, a serial killer, the Nun of Monza, a brilliant work addict, a sister, a vegetarian animal rights activist, and so on; everything could have a masculine version: a male stalker, a man with borderline personality disorder, a man with Asperger's.

Following in this is the hypothesis of Pichón Rivière (1971), that depressive anxieties are the basis of many or all pathologies that arise as reactive and revitalising in respect to the Little Match Girl stage.

I'm going to read some excerpts from a session, where I was reminded of the Little Match Girl, which allowed a patient to think about her status.

The patient walks in and says: "I am late today, just a bit … I had a dream, last night I dreamed of my friend Anna that I have not seen in five years at least; when we were young every time I had to get away from her took a heavy toll on me, I was overwhelmed by a terrible anxiety. Her father had bodyguards, he was under protection because he had been targeted by the Red Brigades … at that time I was overweight, maybe in the dream I was fat and I wore several, really a lot of pairs of underwear over one another."

ME: We have the Red Brigades, we have separations from Anna, perhaps modesty with all those pairs of underwear. Maybe you only need one pair!

PATIENT: The Red Brigades were terrible, it seemed to me that Anna disappeared when she went away, and then I went to the café to pee before coming in. Anna was really beautiful, or at least men liked her. I was always the second choice, no one noticed me.

ME: Well, there is a toilet here that you can use. Then it seems almost as if you feel like a Little Match Girl, a second choice or even a 'no choice'. As for underwear, it seems like an antidote to 'being an easy girl'. I was thinking of a movie, where there were prostitutes in the heat of an island, after all an excited atmosphere, but that ultimately could protect from loneliness and sadness.

PATIENT: Right, but the Little Match Girl is a start already, she must have known a place with a hearth, but the real tragedy is the one described in Svetlana in the poem *The Room*, in which you struggle to find the fourth wall, to get an idea of space; Svetlana had a child with learning disabilities that she had given to an orphanage where he starved to death.

ME: And to think that today you arrived just a bit late.

The patient pointed out to me that before the story of the Little Match Girl, there must be more: the Little Match Girl had to have at least the idea of a "warm hearth", of a "grandmother", though lost and out of reach. A basis for dreaming, for desiring.

> So, we are talking about desire. When my patient Loredana desired me, wanted to make love to me, I was, until yesterday, untroubled: she actually desired her father, whom I was merely the transferential substitute for. Today you tell me that Loredana wants to couple with my mind and that her way of saying it, of a sexual character—"Doctor, I want to make love to you"—is just a linguistic variant. I might even agree, but if Loredana's mind agrees with her "nether regions", and thus Loredana is really determined, is it not difficult for the analyst to take charge of the patient's desire without diverting it transferentially, without bringing up her dad? Should I take her emotion and play with it, help her to transform it? Because, from this perspective, one might wonder whether it is really any different from "actual" love, such as what might bloom with the hairdresser, with whoever will listen to us, whoever understands us and triggers that spark. It's official, I'm panicking now!

Why not just tell Loredana: "Loredana, I wish you knew just how badly I'd want to make love to you! Too bad we met here, and that by the very fact of having met here that is the only thing that we cannot do together!"

Wouldn't it be more honest? Especially if Loredana is actually beautiful. I mean that it's exactly the fact of being there that prevents us from making love to Loredana. If that is the truth, then let us tell it: why am I supposed to talk about her father, Oedipus and counter-Oedipus? The truth is that here we have Loredana who truly loves us, we might fall in love with a patient too, in theory—I can hardly think so because there is the fact of asymmetry and responsibility, so it is like falling in love with one's offspring, it is very unlikely for me—but let's assume that it can happen, at that point being honest is worthwhile. But why do we not make love to Loredana?

Probably because if Loredana had met me at the supermarket, she would have seen but an aging man, that was hardly what Loredana desired; is the fact of being there, and the fact that she felt welcomed, helped, understood, which then made that feeling arise? I would not bring story, or transference, or repetition into this. I would say that Loredana was actually in love, but we cannot do that because we met under the agreement of doing analysis. If this metaphor does not work, I might then tell Loredana: "Loredana, it's like telling your dentist to make love! But I suspect you'd tell that to your dentist just not to get your tooth drilled!"

We always have to find a different and convincing angle. If for example we do not like Loredana at all, we would not say the same things, we would have a different reaction.

Since we cannot mate with the patient, it seems that the highest union allowed to us is being able to stand in at-one-ment where the patient is. Why? To what purpose?

Because I believe that the first need of the patient is to receive a delivery receipt, like the ones post persons bring. If you are a child and you're talking about the detestable teacher who gives you too much homework, it would be nonsensical for me to say to the child: "You're saying you're feeling threatened by me because I give you too many things to think about." The child would think: "Is this guy crazy? It's the teacher I'm worried about!"

Sharing is thus essential, because the patient comes to us and has a problem with his girlfriend, with her husband, with the neighbour, with whatever, but the first thing he needs is to feel that there is someone who puts himself on the same level and shares and understands what he is talking about. So the manifest content is of paramount importance. Logically then for us analysts the manifest content is full of caves in which to build, to search, to settle, to explore, but the first thing is to ensure that the patient feels comprehended in what he is saying, not rejected by way of a "You say this, but you do not realise you're actually talking about this other thing".

> So in theoretical terms, what is this comprehension, which is not just the initial phase of treatment, but through at-one-ment becomes a cornerstone of the analytic work?

I believe that at-one-ment is the process that develops the capacity for containment of the patient, that is, of the container. The development of the container, which is one of the key functions that we analysts have, and the development of the digestive metabolic capacity, that is, of the alpha function and some other function. For now, let us deal with the first two. I think that at-one-ment is realised when you hear the other say something you recognise as the delivery receipt: "He got what I am saying, he understands me!"

The patient says something, and you say something that he feels fits in well with his speech; he feels relieved that he is not alone, that there is someone with him who understands him, otherwise it would be like going to the doctor and saying that you feel a vicious pain to the abdomen, and being told by the doctor: "Open your mouth, I have to take a look at your tonsils." It might be right to have a look at the tonsils, because maybe there were streptococci that had gone down to other parts from the throat, but if a patient tells me that he feels a vicious pain in the stomach, right there I would see it fit to palpate the stomach, see what it feels like, check if the stomach wall reacts, if there is a peritonitis. I'd start from the stomach, even if stomach aches might be epiphenomena of countless other ills that have nothing to do with the stomach, but the patient has to feel that we are like him and that we're not weird wizards doing some mumbo-jumbo. Bion meant this when he talked about extending the field in the sense of interpretations (1963); he meant that if we use interpretation to pull the rabbit out of the hat, we should at least see the rabbit's ears together with the patient.

> How difficult is it and how useful is it not to tell the patient what we understood, keeping the rabbit in the hat?

I believe that we should tell the patient what he can bear to understand, maybe being somewhat disturbed but not over-whelmed by it. Because letting a person in and then letting him leave in a state of shock, such that he might be run over by a car, does not seem like a good thing to me, so I think that sometimes, when we understand first, we should wait and try to understand together. Understanding together would be desirable, though sometimes we might have insights that in the past would have been immediately communicated. We might communicate them even now, but sometimes we understand overly true truths, so we need the time to walk towards them together with the patient, assuming they are really true and that they continue to be so over time, because perhaps in the meantime they are overcome and lose their meaning.

> An American colleague recently mentioned your division of the analyst's mind in two parts: a kitchen where the analyst cooks the patient's answers, and a restaurant where he "serves" interpreta-tions. You then add that the analyst should spend most of his time in the kitchen, measuring out salt, spices, and so on.
>
> How do we understand when it's time to bring out the dishes from the kitchen?

This is really important. I think that, for me, the best way is to share the obvious meaning of the patient's communica-tions. Soon thereafter, I start to cook the manifest material in the kitchen, and when I think it is sufficiently transformed, or cooked, then I serve a small dish. A very small one.

An appetiser?

An appetiser! Just for a start. I offer it to the patient, without compelling him, giving him a chance to taste it. After seeing the patient's reaction, I decide whether I can serve the first course too, and then maybe the second course. With fries, without fries, with more salt or less. I can adjust the dish by listening to the patient's answers to my interventions. In this way there is a continuous flow of work between the kitchen and the restaurant. There is always this flow.

I do not like to formulate interpretations, I rather prefer to offer comments. I offer something to the patient. Then I watch his reaction to my comment-interpretation, and I immediately communicate with the kitchen, where I have to prepare the food: less salt, more sugar, more sauce. I try to keep in harmony with the patient.

> I imagine that all of this has to do with the patient's ability to tolerate what we tell him without experiencing analysis as too painful, right?

Exactly. A problem with which we are often confronted is the emotional voltage tolerable to a patient.

I'm thinking of a patient who worked in a leopard-spot way: an area worked at 3000 volts (in the stories it became the violent tale of an uncle always about to beat or kill his wife), another one at 500 volts (it was the story of an envious co-worker), and then there were areas of low voltage (the cousin who kept withdrawing to play games on the computer), then the friend who never had relationships with anybody but kept looking herself in the mirror, and finally the son who kept playing web games on the smart phone.

These aspects of the self were not "tied" and close to each other as in the leopard's fur, but were unmoored from each other and placed on scenarios that were very distant from and not communicating with each other. So a whole range of possible emotional voltages was present—from the most violently passionate ones to the ones that had an autistic-like taste to them—but broken down into greatly distant geographical areas.

Another mode of voltage adjustment occurred by playing with the session's duration: from an expected fifty minutes to just ten minutes, with the amount of delay alleviating tensions.

All of this is narrated extraordinarily well by Carlo Emilio Gadda in his novel *Un fulmine sul 220*, in which a love story, blossomed at last, comes tragically to an end with an electrical discharge of great power in the electrical substation where the two lovers are relishing their passion for the first time. It is no coincidence that another title by Gadda is *Acquainted with Grief*: to what extent can one be acquainted with grief?

An unavoidable theme is thus that of dosing an "intolerable pain" so that sometimes you have to take action, from the most innocuous measures to those sometimes on the edge of the scale of painkillers, such as the surgeon who sedated himself "with blackberries" of which we spoke above.

> This brings to my mind the matter of the bereavement of reality, the transformation of the session in dream. A few days ago in a seminar a colleague was wondering what was lost, in terms of authentic sharing of grief, during the move "to dream" of life's dramas: I think of a cancer diagnosis, the death of a child, the sudden break-up of a marriage.

To begin with, I think that the first move should always be to stand in at-one-ment with the patient. God forbid I interpreted such a thing, it would be foolish to say to someone who has cancer: "You are feeling something that grows inside you, it's your emotions!", it would be insane. Or I do not know what other foolishness I could say to someone who lost a child. This is why I consider at-one-ment important, it means paying attention to the manifest communication of the patient. That's where we always have to start from. What I am thinking then is something that concerns me alone, and how long I think about that and how much should I share it is something that I need to ponder, then I have to see how the situation is going to evolve. However, what I can do for a patient whose child died, is helping him develop his capacity to metabolise grief, though obviously I cannot give him his son back. I can see if we can tie up other loose ends that he may have left in his life, and that he then neglected because there was a child to look after. The work, in this sense, is an inner work; I can not do anything about reality. If there is a tumour, the place to go to is the oncology department, not my office. But if a patient comes to me and he has cancer I can help him develop those things that allow one to digest tumours, digest the anxiety of death, that is, I can develop his tools for thinking, for suffering, for rejoicing, even though I can not do anything about reality. I can not affect the reality of a person, I can not give him a child, just as I can not introduce him to my cousin, who is still a spinster, with which to have another child. I am useless in reality, but I always have to embrace the patient's perspective from where he is standing. If the patient is hypochondriac and has a liver problem, I have to take a spaceship and fly with him to where his liver is. Our movie opens with two aliens landing on a large reddish mass, which is this planet called liver. There we have to go, so begins the movie, *The Red Planet*. We have to stay on the liver for a while thanks to our negative capability. Then we'll see where we are going to go from there.

Negative capability always reminded me of Socrates' "I know that I know nothing." It is a radically different attitude from the positivism of Freud, who says instead, "… where was the extraneous, the incomprehensible, I have to place my conscious knowledge."

Which is exactly the opposite of what Civitarese says with the idea of *inconsciare*.

I wonder how much do new analysts need to learn to offer concavity to their patients, without continually striving to offer the convexity of interpretation. At the beginning of our career, but not just at the beginning, we are afraid to be sitting there "doing nothing". On the contrary we have to show the patient that we truly have something to say, right? Because anybody can listen!

I think that negative capability is one of Bion's most important concepts. Let us remember that he describes it as the capability to stand in the paranoid-schizoid position without there being any persecution. That is, it is a matter of being capable to be in a mental state of doubt, of not knowing, without feeling threatened, guilty, endangered because of that. To be there, like at the movies, when the screen lights go out or the film breaks, as used to happen in the past, and at that point not to start screaming and calling the fire department, but to sit and wait for someone to re-glue the film and for the movie to go on. Then it might be an even more complex movie, in which the fact that the lights go out is part of the movie itself. How do we know if it is part of the movie or not? We sit there calmly and wait.

We have to wait out the time needed for things to take a definition, a shape. It is as if we witnessed Picasso painting a canvas. Logically we should wait for the canvas to gradually take shape, before doing any work even if tangential, to allow Picasso to keep doing his work. Negative capability is linked to the capability of the analyst—but I would say of the field itself—to be able to dream in session, and by doing so to be able to perform those operations of deconstruction of a symptom that allow to transform it.

So once in a while it's good to shut up!

When we do not understand anything, we can say something just to dress up the situation. I have nothing against silence, if one feels at ease keeping quiet, why not? I'm a talker, it would be very hard for me to keep quiet. It happens to me too, but quite rarely.

> Let us move from a "good" negative thing to a "less good" negative thing. There are few certainties—if one can speak of certainties—guiding us in our work. One that I struggled to conquer is that it is better to bring negative transference to light before it blows up suddenly. Then I read somewhere an interview you gave and now I'm afraid that you want to rob me of this certainty too. Do we have to bring negative transference to light?

There are countless ways to bring it to light.

> I might get off scot-free this time. Yes, because, speaking of global positioning systems, negative transference is a reliable sign that we are entering a dangerous place for analysis, right?

The point is how you bring it to light. I can bring it to light tragically, as in one of those dramas with Irene Papas,[2] or I can bring it to light in another way. I happened to mention that patient who was persecuted by the chief physician, and each time at the beginning of the session there was this chief physician doing terrible things, offending her with every word he said. Then the chief physician too tried to keep as quiet as possible, but he really was the lowest scum, this chief physician: he humiliated her, offended her, hit her. I even tried to say something, to comment on something, to offer an interpretation of transference too, but the following day the chief physician had done even more monstrous things than before, he was a Torquemada. At one point it turned out that this patient had had an idea she really loved, that was to start writing a crime novel on how to kill the chief physician. Then she really started writing that book, inventing some brilliant things. She invented a method of killing him that involved finding out what drugs he took, then searching for common foods, such as grapefruit and so on, that varied the absorption and metabolism of the drug, then she did a computer research until she found the right chemical, and to this day she is writing this crime novel, a series of murders that starts from the murder of the chief physician. Should we take away her enjoyment in doing this? "You are telling me that you fear me so you hate me, you despise me and want to eliminate me from your life." Why, what would be the use? For now let us play "kill the chief physician", which amuses us both, and see where we end up. She may even become a writer, or maybe not. For now we play like that. In short, regarding negative transference, we should have ears for all the different functionings of the patient. The session should always be a poly-ethnic session, in which to account for the patient's poly-ethnicity and our own poly-ethnicity: we are all erotomaniacs, criminals, murderers, likewise the patient. But we only care about a few in this range of characters, otherwise everybody would be everything; we have to see what are the closer identities: if from an Italian identity we come to a Moroccan or Serbian identity we are already expanding the territory, and it is not a given that I have to include the Cambodian one too. We let Pol Pot[3] stay in Cambodia; if by chance he takes the plane and gets closer we take him, but generally I would leave him where he is. Whereas we should try to approach other ethnicities close to our psyche, or at least we should try to have a method for either understanding their language or understanding their workings. As in that case of supervision that I mentioned, in which the colleague approached these incomprehensible Neapolitans. Analysis however is this, analysis is going out and finding out, analysis must be multi-ethnic, that is it should go fetch all the other alien workings that are part of us, if they are already structured, or give them a structure in order to understand them if they are still shapeless.

Here is a question that many already asked you, but I think that when reading any of your books or articles one keeps wondering this, because it has to do with the heart of your work: how do stories cure, what stories cure, and what stories do not cure?

It is not the story that cures, that is, it's not like I can just make up a story and this cures or like I can tell just any story. Stories can be used if they are born to allow the figuration, the representation of something that seethes in the field and that thus finds a way to be said. Keep in mind that today analysis definitely looks more and more to the preverbal, to the pre-symbolic, and to these primitive levels; being able to offer a narrative possibility is a way to make perceptible those needs, fears, and anxieties that were previously below the possibility of being named. Stories by themselves are not curative, they are curative to the extent that they make it possible to catch a few fish, to bring them to light and cook them.

I think that the curative element is the co-construction, done by patient and analyst, of elements that used to be impassable, intransitive, or inexpressible: there is a cure when together with the patient we can weave these elements into a shared narrative. This shared narrative can range from the *transformation in dream*, about which we already talked, to the *transformation in game*. As an example of *transformation in game* I mention that pertaining to playing with the setting, as in the case of the patient who did not want to lie down. But there might also be what I would call a *transformation in biography*, in which I would not bother with checking the element of correspondence with reality or lack thereof—but we have known this for some time now—as much as the work of transformation through which a story that allows to give narratability, visibility, consistency to one's own existence comes to be transformed, created, invented. Today I saw a case of supervision in which there was a rather serious patient, very serious indeed, telling among other things how as a child she, like her brother, had been sodomised by their father. If I start the story from here, basically it's like seeing the second half of a Charles Bronson movie, where violent action is already taking place. If we look at the previous part of the session instead, we see that the beginning was absolutely good, and gradually the analyst had started an increasingly active and increasingly violent interpretive action, with the best intentions; at that point the father who had sodomised the daughter and her brother entered the scene. But does this mean that it is not true that the father had sodomised the daughter as he had done with her brother? I would simply say:

A—We do not know;

B—We have no way of knowing;

C—Nothing could interest us less.

What we do know for certain is that within that field, at some point, a situation was created in which the analyst's interpretations, violent and intrusive, gave life to this piece of transformation in story in which there was a father's violent act and abuse against a daughter. The instant the analyst understands this in *après-coup* he can make a historical novel out of that: that's where the transformation in story as one of the possible transformations is found. The abusive father was born there in that session, sprouted there in that session due to that kind of interpretation.

Could we say that it happened due to the fact that this analyst had taken this violence from the patient and then acted on it, because it was a violence inherent in the patient's history? Yes, we could say so, if this analyst had acted not according to a model which called for a continuous transference interpretation, with an interpretation not linked to the patient's history, but linked to his own history and his own mode of work; so that violence, even if interpretive, was actually the analyst's and there is no doubt that in that situation the abuser was the analyst. So we might have the paradox of a historical reconstruction in which there was an abusive father who in actuality did not commit any abuse; but that's unimportant. What is important is how we manage to turn into a story even the most incredible and least true event, provided that it is consistent, gives firmness, works as a story, is a story that walks with us, is a story with which we can live a free enough future; and it would be better for the patient to experience a non-abusive analyst.

> Here is another question that interests me personally, because it deals with a passion of mine. I love to play games and I played games for a long part of my life, until I had to gradually replace gaming with psychoanalysis and become somewhat serious, as should rightfully be, at least in part. Then I read Ferro talking about transformations in game and of course I wonder if they can be of interest to me. Can you help me better understand what these transformations in game are, what significance might they have in analysis?

I love discovering how certain concepts were born. I have always had an aptitude for playing games in session and, perhaps, even a way of narrating, a way of using my own reverie, a way of making little lights out of it with which to go on; sometimes it is just a linguistic game. But the first time I came up with the concept of transformation in game, was during a supervision in Boston, where there was an analyst past her prime dealing with a very, very lively and quite uncontrollable child. This child had started crafting paper planes—more like paper rockets than planes actually—and started tossing them at this analyst, until one of these planes had hit her in the corner of the eye, hurting her quite a lot. Then, this absolutely composed lady got angry and in turn she started making paper rockets and started tossing them, with ever increasing force, towards the child. It so happened that one of these rockets hit the child right in his eye, in the cornea, and she froze, worried, wondering: "Oh, my God, what am I doing, what have I done?" Then she stopped the game, as the child began swearing at her, with the coarsest and most obscene profanities he knew. This colleague stood for a while as in shock, until she had an absolutely brilliant—I am not sure whether to call it idea—she had an intuitive behaviour, and she began turning this series of profanities into a nursery rhyme. So she started reciprocating this string of profanities like this, putting them into verse and narrating them in the form of a nursery rhyme, rhyming couplets and all. And somehow this child was charmed. After a string of profanities and their rhymes, he said: "My turn now, tell me a lot of bad words, tell me the bad words!" Then she started happily hurling insults, and the child in turn transformed these profanities into a rhyme and directed these verses, like a poem, to the analyst. And this game went on: rather than insulting or hurting each other at that point they were playing "Let's hurl bad words", but in the form of a nursery rhyme.

For the first time it was hard to make the child leave the session, as he kept asking: "More, more!", and then when he left he said: "Yes, I'll go, on condition that tomorrow we keep playing this game!"

And this I find quite extraordinary: a violent game at some point became a fun, harmless game, a game that gradually made it possible to even say bad things. This in turn reminds me of a comment made by Bion in one of his seminars, when he states that we should always, in each session, give the patient a good reason to come back. And I think that fun is a good reason to come back, that is, I think that a good analysis session is a session in which both played together.

This does not mean not being allowed to be serious, or avoiding pain and suffering, but it means that somehow we can play even with pain, with suffering, with grief. We can affect a transformation in drama, a transformation in tragedy, a transformation in any literary form suitable for conveying the kind of emotions that we are trying to bring to life, so as to bring something holographically lively and meaningful within the analytic field, something that the patient will then be able to retain even as a communicative style with himself.

> It seems to me that the risk in this kind of operation, especially for someone who is not well acquainted with the profession, might be to slip into mannerism, possibly ending up being more attentive to the game than to the patient, for example losing sight of the pain. Because one thing is playing a drama, another thing is living it; whether we consider it an actual event or, as you prefer to do, a drama-dream, either way it is a set of emotions that we have to be very cautious to play with. Otherwise there is a risk of standing at such a distance from the patient as to make him feel alone with his own drama, while the analyst is having fun playing on his own.

No, I believe that nobody should play on his own, but rather that there should be a shared game with the patient. Obviously, playing with grief can also mean writing Gadda's *Acquainted with Grief* together: what I am suggesting is not an analysis in the style of Aristophanes, an analysis with a lot of laughs, no, but it is an analysis—to quote Winnicott (1953)—in a transitional space. However, even this definition does not really convey my meaning, maybe I should say an analysis in which there is always a chance to stay mentally alive and never to be paralysed by a concrete fact of life, not even by the most tragic one. That is, it means being able to share with the patient the notion that sometimes in life you can feel like that child in Rossellini's *Germany, Year Zero*, but basically you can start back even from zero, as the film suggests. Obviously, this concept of mine might appear utterly blasphemous, if we think of a situation where there was some pain, some serious grief, some catastrophic grief, but I would think that even in these situations at some point there is something alive that inevitably begins to flow. Even in those situations where pain is really the O, that is, where pain is the central theme that we do not know how to deal with, one of those nameless tragedies that can happen in life, the whole analysis will be centred on how to metabolise this boulder of pain, how to transform it into something that can indeed be dreamed, shared, I would even say played as a game in a lofty sense. Of course, we should always consider that for a child a game is a very serious thing.

I remember that once, for my birthday, I was playing "American Indians" with other children, and I was all dressed up as an Indian, and then my aunt, who was very dear to me, walked up to me with a t-shirt—which by the way I really liked—to size it up on my shoulders. To me that was a terrible insult, that someone would dare lay a t-shirt on the Indian chief's shoulders, because it disrupted the game, and I remember that I had a terrible fit of anger, because it was like violating the movie that I was creating for the game.

> Here I do humanity a favour, with a question that avenges all the times we read: "We have to stay on O," "We have to achieve O." To those who have yet to properly process Bion, and thus need your beginners' notes, how does Antonino Ferro explains this O?

Well, O is the thing itself, the unknowable thing, it is the underlying reason why a patient is in analysis, it is the structuring identity, and it is something that we will never know. None of us knows what his own O is, and I would say that, all in all, in my life I have hardly ever witnessed a transformation in O. I remember only one transformation that did not pass through knowledge or a quantifiable emotion, but that instead amounted to a quantum leap in mental growth, as a transformation in O should be. This was a patient with a two-dimensional mental space, an adhesive woman who had no idea of three-dimensionality, and it happened the day when from a two-dimensional view of reality she discovered and adopted a three-dimensional view, when she discovered that there was a third dimension and things no longer appeared two-dimensional, flat to her. The world opened up to her under this new measure of depth, and she felt the same with respect to herself and to her emotional life.

I think that the most brilliant thing in O was written by Grotstein, an author I love very much, when he said that O has to be transformed within category two on Bion's grid. Let me explain; O has to be progressively dreamed: we will never know the real O, we will always know its derivatives, which will take the form of a lie. In other words O has to undergo a *transformation in lie*, which makes it tolerable: we can never know the ultimate reality of our own emotion, our own need, our own anxiety, our own fear, our own way of being, if not by exceptional circumstances; we will always know its diluted aspects, such as the ones we can create with dream or with the creativity of a dialogue, in analysis or with a person that is significant to us. We will be able to approach truth, but any truth, in order to be witnessed, shared, or experienced, needs some room for lies around it. Truth without a handle of lies would look like a hot frying pan that someone asked us to hold, while inside it fries are sizzling in steaming oil and the temperature is unapproachable: we need that handle of lies in order to pick up the pan and the truth (and the excellent fries that truth offers us).

Our species cannot tolerate the harsh, hard impact with reality. Bion repeatedly accuses Klein of not understanding that, when he said he had died in the Battle of Amiens,[4] he was not using a metaphor: he did not want to express a situation of grief, he did not want to talk about the agony and how that had radically changed him, rather he meant to tell Klein that he had died. Klein never understood what that meant, and surely neither do I understand what Bion meant. Bion's O regarding Amiens is that he died there; we do not understand, moreover it's an experience we can maybe have once and a half in life, if we are lucky, to be dead yet to be alive and happy. So we approach with our oven mitts made of metaphors, of lies, meaning by "lie" the softening, the mitigation of ultimate knowledge.

Notes

1. George Devereux was a Hungarian anthropologist and psychoanalyst, who did field research among various indigenous peoples.

2. Irene Papas is a famous Greek actress whose long movie career spans the twentieth century.

3. Pol Pot was a Cambodian revolutionary, leading the Khmer Rouge guerrillas, who became dictator of Cambodia between 1976 and 1979.

4. The brutal battle of Amiens began on August 8, 1918, and launched the final Allied offensive against the Central Powers. Twenty-one-year-old Bion commanded a section of tanks, which represented an innovation in First World War. Several years later, Bion uttered the terrible and paradoxical statement that this immersion in war had killed him. In *The Long Weekend* (1982) he writes: "They have a way of making people look so life-like, but really we are dead. I? Oh yes, I died—on August 8, 1918" (p. 265). In *A Memoir of the Future* (1991) one of the characters representing Bion says: "I would not go near the Amiens-Roye road for fear I should meet my ghost—I died there" (p. 257).

CHAPTER TEN

Meetings

S ince you mentioned him and he passed away not long ago, I'd like to ask you to tell us something about James Grotstein.

When I think about Jim Grotstein, I can't help but instinctively smile, because he was a kind person, an extremely generous person, a person who did not realise just how brilliant he was and how many turning points he allowed psychoanalysis to reach, so I'd like to commemorate his generosity, the utter absence of both assertiveness and of that pride that sometimes can, in particular minds, even come with disdain towards those who are less brilliant. Also, his boundless affection and sweetness. Then I'd like to recall two things: the first is the applause that greeted him after the wonderful speech he had given at the conference on Bion in Boston and the standing ovation that was accorded him with true affection (Grotstein, 2009). Grotstein had a great capacity to give, to share, to be untroubled by those who would appropriate one of his ideas and claim it as their own; he had no sense of possession, of owning ideas, regarding which he thought the more one shares them, the more they grow: no property rights. And then I remember how we went to eat at the restaurant together, and how he had walked a long stretch of one of Boston's main streets without noticing that he still had a napkin in front of his trousers, sort of like an apron, and how he walked completely unaware of his apron, until, after more than an hour, we noticed the napkin with which he was going around. Then he took it off and placed it on his shoulder, and kept walking like nothing happened. So, about him I would like to remember his utter lack of a "I am Grotstein": "I am nobody!"

Let us talk about clinical practice. Presently psychoanalysis is focused on defects of symbolisation, more or less, both in so-called neurotic patients and in more fragile patients. How can we help them?

Do we still have to use the concept of symbolisation?

To be on the same page!

Or maybe we should dare to change the language already, at least between experts. Of course there is English that, as long as one can speak it fluently or at least a bit, allows everybody to share things, and then it is better to speak it, so we can understand each other even when we're talking about symbolisation.

However, perhaps it might be possible to speak of transformation of alpha elements, to speak of the vicissitudes of the container, that is, to express the same things in a different and in some ways more accurate language, because it is better at pointing out where the problem lies; namely, whether it is an excess of beta elements, or a lacking alpha function; it is a bit like going from an optical microscope to an electron microscope, which shows us exactly where the cell membrane we are talking about is.

A couple of tips for working with a patient who has a borderline functioning?

Watch a good movie where the cowboys struggle to drive a herd of cattle across the river, that is, understand that here one has to start from a "cowboy" function.

That's it.

Right! There is a cowboy movie with these huge herds that do not want to cross the river at all, so the herders have to learn how to contain them, how to tame a horse. With a borderline patient we are always more or less in a Western movie, *High Noon* showdowns, or we stand there seeing what movie the patient will offer us and how we might start to shoot it.

However, we should keep in mind that borderline is a category of the psychic. We all have borderline areas with which we should have a passable relationship: that is, we should be able to open an embassy in our borderline areas, one in our psychotic areas, at least a consulate in autistic areas, another in psychosomatic areas; my point is, we should not assume that there is a mental functioning that is alien to us.

Regarding autism, previously you mentioned the Italian Ministry of Health guidelines that effectively ousted psychoanalysis and more from the cure of autism. What happened and what can be done to prevent such a situation from occurring again?

I think that certainly there were mistakes on the part of psychoanalysis. Instead of learning to say "I do not know," once again we said "I know, I know it well, let me explain it." There are areas of the mind that we are still unable to cure; we struggle to take care of, and to be able to somehow relieve, suffering located in those areas. So I cannot tell a patient diagnosed as schizophrenic that by doing analysis he is definitely going to feel better, I have to tell him to what extent today we are able to work. And certainly, regarding autistic children, we probably know more in terms of research than in terms of effective therapeutic power, so we have to be cautious before issuing proclamations.

Then, if we are talking about Ministry regulations, I'd say that when Hurricane Katrina comes, they're going to get soaked, so I would not bother about that. Surely it was a failure for psychoanalysis to say that it can understand everything, cure everything. Psychoanalysis is not able to cure and heal everything. There are things that it can do more successfully; I think there are people who have made a good analysis and have improved significantly compared to their autistic nuclei. We should not forget that we all have autistic nuclei, and that there are even children who were saved from an autistic state. Probably not many, I think, largely because of lacking a model more than lacking a method. There are models that are still totally inadequate for ills so alien compared to our normal way of functioning. Let's say we still do not know much, but if I had to start an analysis today—something I'm not going to do because the first time was enough for me—I would be most interested in working on autistic nuclei, without a doubt. Not on Oedipus, for sure.

I think that in the future psychoanalysis will deal with areas of autistic functioning and with autistic patients again—so I anticipate—and will reap significant victories. I think it will be a very effective therapeutic tool.

But first some ways to conceive analysis have to change; for example, the habit to continually interpret autistic children is not just totally foolish, but also absolutely iatrogenic, it makes them become ill. Surely it is a matter of working in new ways that are just now beginning to be shared by some.

Are there possible areas of application of the field model in psychiatric institutions, outside the consulting room?

Strictly speaking, I would not apply psychoanalysis to anything outside the consulting room and outside analysis itself. I understand that this is a radical stance, even though during my training I had the peculiar experience of working in a psychiatric clinic in which both the director and his aide were psychoanalysts, De Martis and Petrella. I have to say that day to day work was not any different, that is, we acted as psychiatrists to the patient, to whom we gave no interpretations, but certainly the atmosphere was analytic, in the sense of the importance of human respect, of containment, of going somewhat beyond appearances and symptoms.

Indeed, I believe that we should not be as radical as I am; I think that psychoanalysts in a public healthcare institution might work better than others who are not analysts, thanks to a certain ability to listen, a certain ductility, a certain acquaintance with areas of the mind we usually recoil from. So I think that a level of resonance with some aspects of psychoanalysis can be found in healthcare institutions. I think this is the maximum width psychoanalysis can reach. There have been and there are still psychiatric institutions in which there was a strong psychoanalytic model: there used to be Chestnut Lodge in Rockville, Maryland, now there is Austen Riggs in Stockbridge, Massachusetts, where there is a psychoanalytic model and patients undergo analysis within the institution, participate in groups with the staff, and the activity is strongly analytically oriented. I think it is the last institution of its kind left, but it works!

Do you think that the dialogue between psychoanalysis and neuroscience is useful, or do you see them as two worlds that can progress in parallel and hardly ever intersect?

I would answer in a radical way: they seem to me like two fascinating parallel worlds, each of which should walk its own path. Psychoanalysis is a discipline that has nothing to do with neuroscience. If then we want to make them talk to each other, we can do it, because perhaps some people want to discover the functioning of the limbic areas, and this makes them happy, and maybe they are happier if it is confirmed that dreaming activity really occurs even while we are awake, and so on.

I would leave everybody free to dialogue with whoever they want: if an analyst is pleased to work better by borrowing concepts from neuroscience, geography, or cuisine, let him do it freely. I would not forbid anybody from doing something that is useful for him at that time. If I had to tell you whether I personally need to read about neurobiology, as an analyst I do not need it at all, as a person living in 2016 on the other hand I do, because those are things that pique my curiosity, just like I'm curious about the concept of black holes. But I have my doubts that a black hole has something to do with psychoanalysis. Except as a metaphor, of course.

> During these three meetings we had, a swallow built a nest in the gutter and now there's the sweet tweet of swallow chicks coming from the outside just as we are speaking. How important is it to reserve a question for these birds, even though they are outside our office and outside the field of psychoanalysis?

Well, I hope that birds can always hatch from their eggs and find a nest. Then, I wish that there were not just birds that make a sweet tweet but also birds that make a swear-tweet. A terrible fear I have is that psychoanalysis becomes "normotyping", something that only allows you to be "sweet". I wish there was a balanced alternation between "swearing" and "sweeting" that makes life worth living, that is, without necessarily having to be iconoclasts, but without having to continuously repeat the *Kyrie eleison, Christe eleison,* the celebration of a rite, either.

> To close our interview, I borrow a question from a Brazilian[1] colleague and ask you what are your hopes for the future of psychoanalysis: what perspectives and what challenges lie ahead?

I wish psychoanalysis a hundred, another hundred, and a hundred more years of life. I am a bit worried because sometimes it risks continually repeating itself, while I think that we should bury many concepts that in clinical practice are no longer useful. We should have the courage to discard what we no longer need to use totally new tools, techniques, methods, ideas, some of which may even be revolutionary. I expect good sense to prevail, I expect that is possible, instead of witnessing the death of a psychoanalysis sometimes immobilised by a "Jurassic" protocol, to continue to see it thrive, once again transformed into something alive and totally creative. I remember that at the last IPA Congress in Prague I said that I was tired of thinking of psychoanalysis as a tool that served to translate the things said in one language into another language, as we had been allowed to do by the Rosetta Stone, in which the same sentence was written in hieroglyphs, Demotic script, and Ancient Greek, and this allowed us to decipher the meaning of hieroglyphs. Today I would no longer think of psychoanalysis as something that can decrypt and convey a message in a different language, but I would be happy to see the Rosetta Stone broken, smashed to pieces, and put in an oven to see what comes out when it is properly cooked.

Note

1. For further details refer to Rosângela de Oliveira Faria's interview, that should be published on *Berggasse 19*, biannual journal of the Brazilian Psychoanalytic Society of Ribeirão Preto.

REFERENCES

Adams, D. (1979). *The Hitchhiker's Guide to the Galaxy*. London: Pan.

Aguayo, J., & Malin, B. (2013). *Wilfred Bion: Los Angeles Seminars and Supervision*. London: Karnac.

Baranger, M., & Baranger, W. (1961–1962). La situacion analitica como campo dinamico. *Revista Uruguaya de Psicoanálisis*, 4(1): 3–54.

Bion, W. R. (1959). Attacks on linking. *International Journal of Psychoanalysis*, 40: 308–315.

Bion, W. R. (1962). *Learning from Experience*. London: Heinemann.

Bion, W. R. (1963). *Elements of Psycho-analysis*. London: Heinemann.

Bion, W. R. (1967). Notes on memory and desire. *Psychoanalytic Forum*, 2: 272–273, 279–280.

Bion, W. R. (1970). *Attention and Interpretation*. London: Tavistock.

Bion, W. R. (1974). *Brazilian Lectures. Revised and corrected edn.* London: Karnac, 1990.

Bion, W. R. (1982). *The Long Weekend: 1897–1919 (Part of a Life)*. Abingdon, UK: Fleetwood Press.

Bion, W. R. (1991). *A Memoir of the Future*. London: Karnac.

Bion, W. R. (2005a). *The Tavistock Seminars*. London: Karnac.

Bion, W. R. (2005b). *The Italian Seminars*. London: Karnac.

Bleger, J. (1967). *Symbiosis and Ambiguity*. London: Routledge, 2013.

Bolognini, S. (1991). The analyst's affects: analysis by the ego and analysis by the self. *Rivista Psicoanalitica, 37*: 339–371.

Bolognini, S. (2008). *Secret Passages*. London: Routledge, 2010.

Calvino, I. (1965). The origin of the birds. In: *T Zero*. New York: Harcourt, Brace & World, 1969.

Choder-Goldman, J. (2016). Global perspectives: an interview with Antonino Ferro. *Psychoanalytic Perspectives, 13*: 129–143.

Civitarese, G. (2014). *I sensi e l'inconscio*. Rome: Borla.

Civitarese, G. (2015). Transformations in hallucinosis and the receptivity of the analyst. *International Journal of Psychoanalysis, 96*: 1091–1116.

Corrao, F. (1986). *Il concetto di campo come modello teorico*. In: *Orme (vol. 2)*. Milan, Italy: Cortina, 1998.

Etchegoyen, H. (1986). *The Fundamentals of Psychoanalytic Technique*. London: Karnac, 2005.

Freud, S. (1918b). From the History of an Infantile Neurosis. *S. E., 17*: 1–124. London: Hogarth.

Grotstein, J. S. (1981). *Do I Dare Disturb the Universe? A Memorial to Wilfred R. Bion*. Beverly Hills, CA: Caesura.

Grotstein, J. S. (2009). Dreaming as a "curtain of illusion": Revisiting the "royal road" with Bion as our guide. *International Journal of Psychoanalysis, 90*: 733–752.

Joseph, B. (1985). Transference: the total situation. *International Journal of Psychoanalysis, 66*: 447–454.

Laplanche, J., & Pontalis, J.-B. (1973). *The Language of Psycho-Analysis*. New York: Hogarth.

Merleau-Ponty, M. (1945). *Phenomenology of Perception*. London: Routledge & Kegan Paul, 1962.

Nissim Momigliano, L. (2001). *L'Ascolto Rispettoso. Scritti psicoanalitici*. Milan, Italy: Cortina.

Ogden, T. H. (1994). The concept of interpretive action. *Psychoanalytic Quarterly, 63*: 219–245.

Pichón Rivière, E. (1971). *El Proceso Grupal: del Psicoanalisis a la Psicologia Social*. Buenos Aires: Nueva Vision.

Quinodoz, J. M. (2004). *Reading Freud*. London: Routledge, 2005.

Stern, D. B. (2015). *Relational Freedom. Properties of the Interpersonal Field.* London: Routledge.

Thomä, H., & Kächele, H. (1988). *Psychoanalytic Practice. Vol. 2. Clinical Studies.* Lanham, MD: Jason Aronson, 1994.

Winnicott, D. W. (1953). Transitional Objects and Transitional Phenomena—A Study of the First Not-Me Possession. *International Journal of Psychoanalysis, 34*: 89–97.

Winnicott, D. W. (1960). The theory of the parent-infant relationship. *International Journal of Psychoanalysis, 41*: 585–595.

INDEX